Monasticism: A Very Short Introduction

VERY SHORT INTRODUCTIONS are for anyone wanting a stimulating and accessible way into a new subject. They are written by experts, and have been translated into more than 45 different languages.

The series began in 1995, and now covers a wide variety of topics in every discipline. The VSI library now contains over 500 volumes—a Very Short Introduction to everything from Psychology and Philosophy of Science to American History and Relativity—and continues to grow in every subject area.

Very Short Introductions available now:

Available soon:

For more information visit our website

www.oup.com/vsi/

Stephen J. Davis

MONASTICISM

A Very Short Introduction

OXFORD
UNIVERSITY PRESS

Great Clarendon Street, Oxford, OX2 6DP,
United Kingdom

Oxford University Press is a department of the University of Oxford.
It furthers the University's objective of excellence in research, scholarship,
and education by publishing worldwide. Oxford is a registered trade mark of
Oxford University Press in the UK and in certain other countries

Published in the United States of America by Oxford University Press
198 Madison Avenue, New York, NY 10016, United States of America

British Library Cataloguing in Publication Data
Data available

Library of Congress Control Number: 2017948017

ISBN 978-0-19-871764-5

Printed in Great Britain by
Ashford Colour Press Ltd, Gosport, Hampshire

Links to third party websites are provided by Oxford in good faith and
for information only. Oxford disclaims any responsibility for the materials
contained in any third party website referenced in this work.

Contents

Acknowledgements

I must begin by thanking my Coptic Orthodox monastic friends in Egypt, especially those in the Monasteries of the Syrians, the Monastery of St Bishoi, and the White Monastery, who have shown me such generous hospitality over the past decade and have demonstrated to me what it means to live in that delicate balance between a solitary and communal life. *Shukran, yā abā'inā!* Many thanks as well to the team at Oxford University Press, led by Andrea Keegan and Jenny Nugee, the commissioning editors for the VSI series. I benefited tremendously from the input generously offered by OUP's editorial and expert readers. I also want to acknowledge Yale University for the funding that facilitated research trips to sites and collections in Egypt, England, France, Ireland, Israel-Palestine, Italy, and Scotland.

I am cognizant of my indebtedness to scholarly friends and colleagues who fielded my many questions and devoted their time and energy to reading my work and offering feedback. Special gratitude goes to Phyllis Granoff, Eric Greene, Katie Lofton, and Andy Quintman for their critical eyes and personal support. In particular, the opportunity to co-teach a Yale course with Andy on the subject of 'Monasticism in Comparative Perspective' was an absolutely indispensable part of this process. At an early stage, it allowed me the chance to flesh out my ideas about the structure and content of the book in close conversation with him and a brilliant group of undergraduate students. It was an honour to teach with him: I have learned much from his pedagogy and scholarship.

This project has witnessed many life changes. I signed the contract for this book in November 2013, shortly after my term as Head of Pierson College at Yale began. I want to thank my students and colleagues at Pierson for providing me with my own sort of cloister, a home space where their daily acts of kindness and shared commitment to inclusiveness sustain and inspire me to forms of service I wouldn't be capable of otherwise. Now, three and a half years later, my three children have all left home for their own college study and for paths beyond, and my wife Jenny and I find ourselves adjusting to an empty nest (albeit thankfully with over 500 Pierson friends to cushion the blow). Through it all, Jenny has been my rock, my compass, and my constant companion. This book, along with all the others, is dedicated to her.

Stephen J. Davis
1 January 2017

List of illustrations

List of abbreviations

EM   *Encyclopedia of Monasticism*, ed. W. M. Johnston, 2 vols (Chicago: Fitzroy Dearborn, 2000)

NPNF   *A Select Library of the Nicene and Post-Nicene Fathers*, ed. P. Schaff (New York: Christian Literature Co., 1886–90; reprinted, Peabody, MA: Hendrickson, 1994)

YMAP   Yale Monastic Archaeology Project

Introduction

Aṭ-ṭuyūr! Imbāriḥ billīl kānū biyaklū mukhī!
The birds! Last night they were eating my brain!

This exclamation came from the mouth of a Coptic monk as we sat
together sipping tea during a break from work in December 2014.
His words, so full of concern, were followed almost immediately
by his characteristic welcoming smile and hearty laugh. We were
sitting in a small kitchen, on the second floor of the library at the
Monastery of the Syrians, located in the desert west of the Nile
Delta in northern Egypt.

My monastic friend—for the purposes of this book, he has asked to
remain anonymous—is an Egyptian in his mid-to-late forties, a short,
squat man with a wispy black beard flecked with grey. He wears a
typical Coptic monk's attire: a black robe, black canvas moccasins,
and a black hood with golden crosses stitched into the fabric. In the
monastic library, he helps manage one of the largest manuscript
collections in the country, an archive of around 1,000 texts written
in several languages (Syriac, Coptic, Arabic, Ethiopic) and dating
from the 5th or 6th century CE to the present.

But today, his mind is elsewhere. 'The birds! Last night they were
eating my brain!' He is using a metaphor to describe his nightly
struggle with distracting thoughts. The thoughts that interrupt

his prayer and sleep are experienced as unwanted external forces: they are like the birds of the air, pecking at his concentration and fraying his treasured quietude. His monastery is home to over 300 Arabic-speaking Egyptian monks, but within the community he lives alone in a mud-brick residence outside the monastery's walls. By day, he works in the library, welcomes visitors, and when able attends the designated hours of prayer (6.00 am, 9.00 am, 12.00 noon, 3.00 pm, 5.00 pm, and 6.00 pm). At night, he prepares his own simple evening meal and does battle with the birds.

At first glance, my monastic friend seems a host of contradictions. He is a gregarious solitary, a light-hearted soul who takes his spiritual struggles with the utmost seriousness. He embraces guests with a warm and genuine hospitality, yet he constantly yearns to retreat to his cell, or to be taken up to heaven to be with God (*Khudñi, yā rabb!* 'Take me, Lord!'). He avoids talk of his family background and his former life, but he beams with pride when his ten-year-old nephew visits. He eschews use of a mobile phone, but at the same time he is occasionally curious and full of questions about what is going on outside the gates of his community. He is self-effacing, readily deferring to others, never drawing undue attention to himself, but when I ask to take his picture, it is clear he is touched that I would want to capture his image as a keepsake. In the photo, one side of his face is in shadow, the other in light. He smiles and the dancing lines of crow's feet crease his skin. His eyes are a pool of calm.

In many ways, this brief portrait of a practising monk is a suitable place to begin a *Very Short Introduction* to the practice of monasticism. Ultimately, the monastic vocation (Christian, Buddhist, or otherwise) is about persons choosing to live an alternative lifestyle—monks, nuns, and communities who see themselves pursuing a path that is defined in opposition to, and yet still crucially related to, the patterns and predilections of everyday society. Part of my task in this book is to make sense of this contrariness, and of the diverse and constructive ways that

Monasticism

2

the monastic life has come to expression from its ancient origins to the 21st century.

My goal will be to present an accessible account that addresses basic questions about monastic social forms and spirituality. What is monasticism and how is it distinguished from other kinds of religious and non-religious practice? What is our earliest evidence for monasticism and what different types have developed from antiquity to the present day? How are monastic communities organized and how are aspects of life like food, sleep, sex, work, and prayer regimented? What do stories about saints communicate about monastic identity and ethics? Where and in what kinds of physical settings are monasteries located, and how do these settings impact the everyday life and worldview of the monks and nuns who dwell there? Finally, what place is there for monasticism in the modern world?

In trying to answer these questions, I will draw on three kinds of evidence. First, as a historian, I will investigate ancient and medieval textual sources to give my readers a sense of how monasticism developed in its classical forms of expression; in addition, I will also draw on my study of contemporary monks and monastic communities to give a picture of how monasticism is lived today. Second, as a scholar trained in religious studies, I will engage with literature and art as a means for exploring the theologies and lived values that have motivated and sustained monastic communities through the centuries. Third, as an archaeologist, I will rely on my knowledge of material culture to provide a picture of how physical places and objects have conditioned monastic practice. In my view, exploring the materialities of monastic practice is essential for understanding the way that different forms of monastic spirituality operate. One of the things that will make this book distinctive is the way that it investigates monasticism in and through its embodied contexts. With these approaches in mind, then, let us begin our task by defining the term 'monasticism' itself.

Chapter 1
Definitions

The word 'monasticism'—like all others ending with the suffix 'ism'—is in fact of modern coinage. Its French equivalent (*monachisme*) first makes its appearance in the 16th century CE, while in English one of the earliest scholarly writers to employ the term was Joseph Milner in his four-volume work, *The History of the Church of Christ*, published in 1795. Milner's anti-Catholic perspective on the subject was decidedly hostile: he lamented the rise of early Christian monasticism and associated it with moral 'vices' and 'degeneracy'. And yet, despite its origins as a negative epithet, the word would later become appropriated as a neutral or positive term of description, applied not only to Catholic and Orthodox Christian forms of practice, but to Buddhist, Jain, and other religious traditions as well. But to what, exactly, does the term refer?

The roots of the word are found in the Greek language. 'Monasticism' derives from the Greek adjectives *monos* ('solitary, alone'), or its cognate *monachos* ('solitary, deserted'). Our first evidence for the use of *monachos*, or the feminine form *monachē*, to refer to a Christian monk or nun comes from an Egyptian papyrus dated to June 324 CE. The document records a legal complaint registered by a certain Dioscorus Caeso against his neighbours, Pamounis and Harpalus, whose cows had damaged his plantings and prevented his own cattle from grazing. When

Dioscorus caught one of the cows in the act, Pamounis and Harpalus allegedly attacked him with a club, threw him to the ground, and beat him up. In the complaint about this assault, Dioscorus credits 'the deacon Antonius and the monk Isaac' for rescuing him and saving his life. In this case, the 'solitary' in question seems to have been someone actually living in a village or town, not isolated in some remote location. Later, *monachos* would come to be applied as a broad term used to refer to monastics of any stripe, from solitary (or semi-solitary) renunciants to those living under a common rule in walled communities.

In late antiquity, the matter was complicated by the use of at least four other terms to refer to persons who dedicated themselves to a life marked as different in some way from the conventional routines of the Graeco-Roman household and civic society. The first was *apotactite* (Greek, *apotaktikos*, 'one who has been set apart'), a designation that originally seems to have been applied to monastics living in urban and village households, but later came to describe a range of monastic lifestyles. The second was *anchorite* (Greek, *anachōrētēs*, 'one who has withdrawn'), a term that typically referred to monastics who had physically retreated from society to live in isolation. The third was *cenobite* (Greek, *koinobiōtēs*, 'one who lives in a community'), which was applied to monastics who chose to live with other monastics in a designated space called a 'monastery'. The fourth was *ascetic* (Greek, *askētēs*, 'one who trains in a discipline'), a term used even before the rise of formalized monastic communities to refer to individuals who engaged in rigorous practices of renunciation pertaining to money, food, sex, and other worldly attachments. By the 4th century, the term 'ascetic' naturally came to be applied to persons living in monasteries as well as those who engaged in more solitary acts of self-abnegation.

The terms surveyed here—monastic, apotactite, anchorite, cenobite, and ascetic—capture five important characteristics relevant to our understanding of monasticism as it developed in the Greek-speaking world of early Christianity: solitude, the status of being set apart, withdrawal, community, and discipline. This fluidity in terminology (as well as some of the inherent incongruities) reflected a situation of variability and flux in the early history of Christian monasticism.

Such diversity of practice was in fact a point of considerable concern for some early church leaders, who made efforts to canonize the forms they favoured and condemn those they did not. In the late 4th century, one such leader was a man named Jerome (c.347–420 CE) who styled himself a spiritual advisor to monastic women. In a letter written in the year 384 to a nun named Eustochium, Jerome endorsed only two kinds of monastic practice (belonging to what he called 'two classes of monks'): the solitary life (belonging to anchorites) and the communal life (belonging to cenobites). In stark contrast, he vilified a third type: 'those who live in twos and threes, but seldom in larger numbers, and are bound by no rule, but do exactly as they choose'.

The third type of monasticism he describes resembles quite closely the kind of village or urban monasticism for which we have some of our earliest evidence—not only the monk Isaac who saved Dioscorus Caeso and the 'apotactites' commemorated in papyri, but also well-documented female ascetics who lived ascetic lives in their own households. In Jerome's eyes (and those of some early Christian bishops), such small groups of monks and nuns were dangerous—not bound by a common rule and thus harder to control by the church hierarchy.

A little later, two monastic rulebooks written in 6th-century Italy—*The Rule of the Master* and *The Rule of St Benedict*—would also condemn wandering ascetics, who operated outside the lines of ecclesiastical jurisdiction and were thus viewed as worthy of suspicion. In the end, however, such efforts by leaders to squelch heterodox forms of monasticism provide us with valuable historical evidence for an early Christian monastic landscape populated by a diverse range of lifestyles and practices.

Such variations and shifting self-definitions are also evidenced in the (even earlier) history of Buddhist monasticism in India, where a very different linguistic context poses its own challenges as we try to determine English terminological equivalents and draw comparisons to monasticism in the Greek Mediterranean world. Unlike in the case of ancient Christianity, where it took over three centuries from the death of Jesus for a monastic movement to emerge, early Buddhist sources associate the rise of monastic communities and practices with the lifetime of the Buddha himself. Born as Siddhartha Gautama, the Buddha was granted his honorific title (meaning 'the Awakened One') after his experience of enlightenment. While there is debate over the chronology of his life, he probably lived in the 5th century BCE in the Ganges River basin in north-eastern India and died *c.*410 BCE.

A key source for the Buddha's biography and for the origins and early terminology of Buddhist monasticism is the *Vinaya Piṭaka*, part of the Buddhist scriptural canon written down 400–500 years after his death and preserved in the Pāli language. The title *Vinaya Piṭaka* means 'basket of discipline', and the written collection it designates includes both narrative material on the Buddha's life and sets of rules designed to regulate the conduct of his monastic followers.

One section of the *Vinaya* describes Buddha's founding of a *sangha*, a word in Pāli and Sanskrit typically translated as 'monastic community'. The text describes how, after his experience of enlightenment, five followers came to him, each requesting permission to be ordained as a 'monk' (Pāli, *bhikkhu*; Sanskrit, *bhikṣu*). The ordination described is notable for its simplicity: the Buddha says, 'Come, monk', and invites each of them to undertake the religious life in order to overcome suffering. Over time, the original five followers were joined by five others, and they were all sent out into the world and authorized to ordain others using a slightly more elaborate formula: 'I go for refuge to the Buddha. I go for refuge to the doctrine (Pāli, *dhamma*; Sanskrit, *dharma*).

I go for refuge to the community (*sangha*).' Thus, as framed by this foundation story, the identity of the monastic community was conditioned by two factors especially: itinerancy (a status of wandering homelessness) and the vows of ordination.

Later, when certain problems arose in the regulation of discipline within the community, the ordination ceremony was expanded, and supplemented by an elaborate system of rules touching on matters ranging from possessions and clothing to food and sex. In the *Vinaya*, the elaboration of this monastic system is described as being instituted by the Buddha in stages, in the form of restrictions and allowances developed in response to specific situations. Wandering monks were granted the opportunity to take up temporary refuge at forest retreats during the rainy seasons, and eventually some of these centres developed into year-round residences. The periodic retreat centres and permanent residences were designated by the Pāli term, *vihāra* ('monastery'). Meanwhile, the monastic regimen described in the *Vinaya* came to include separate sets of vows for novices (thirty-six vows) and for fully ordained monks (253 vows). In the beginning, the Buddha allegedly did not support the idea of women's ordination, but the *Vinaya Piṭaka* tells the story of how he changed his mind and allowed for the ordination of Buddhist nuns as a concession, as long as they adhered to a more restrictive set of 364 vows.

At their common core, the vows for monks, novices, and nuns include admonitions against killing, stealing, sexual intercourse, lying, drinking alcohol, wearing flowers or perfume, singing or dancing, sleeping in a luxurious bed, eating at an improper time, and possessing valuables. But women's monastic ordination came with extra conditions. These are summed up in the so-called 'Eight Revered Precepts', or Eight *Garudhammas*, a set of additional requirements for female monastics preserved in a story, probably apocryphal, about how the Buddha authorized the ordination of women while insisting on their subordination to male monks. This subordination is spelled out in terms of social

8

deference to monks of all ages (Precept 1), dependence on male monastic orders for administrative oversight and ritual leadership (Precepts 2–6), and the disavowal of any right to admonish or instruct a monk (Precepts 7–8).

A couple of final observations about the *Vinaya*. First, as in the case of early Christian monasticism, one observes fluidity and diversity in the shaping of early Buddhist monastic community. Alongside monastic itinerancy, temporary and permanent settlements developed in which monks took up residence. The text also witnesses an expanding structure of vows and the conditional authorization of women's communities. These changes and developments are all attributed to the personal agency of the Buddha; however, given the gap between his lifetime and the written publication of the *Vinaya*, it is quite likely that these stories and rules collections have, at least in part, a retrospective function and that the Buddha's life story dramatizes institutional developments that continued after his death.

Second, despite the chronological complexities of the *Vinaya*, the collection still tells us quite a lot about the early formation of Buddhist monastic identity. The community of monks and nuns is seen to be authorized by the Buddha's own person. It is conditioned by acts of wandering and refuge-taking. It is grounded in the ritual of ordination and the recitation of vows. And it involves adherence to disciplinary regimens of the body.

My introductory discussion and comparison of key terms and themes in ancient Greek and Indian sources raises vexing questions about definitions. What do we mean when we use the term 'monasticism' and apply it to the very different cultural and linguistic contexts of early Christianity and Buddhism, let alone to other historical and religious settings not yet addressed? How can we responsibly go about this task without succumbing to what Jacques Derrida called 'globalatinization'—a colonialist, comparativist approach that mutely 'assumes a translatability of language, concepts, culture, religion, [etc.]…that in fact resist translation'? How do we avoid forms of cultural appropriation within an academic landscape where the Latinized term 'monasticism' is already widely used to categorize non-Western religious practices? In short, how do we resist the tendency to view the multiplicity of global practices typically identified as 'monastic' through a Western (predominantly Christian) lens? In light of these problems, is this term sufficient to the task of describing such diversity and flux?

There are no quick fixes or easy solutions to this dilemma. In a book entitled *Monasticism: A Very Short Introduction*, we certainly remain constrained in part by the terminology we inherit. But I think we can at least move towards a more nuanced perspective by attending to various local terminologies and sets of practices, and by marking the term 'monasticism' itself as an imperfect act of cultural translation that sometimes obscures as much as it reveals.

As in the case of other definitional terms, it is not surprising to find some ambiguity and inconsistency in the way that scholars have used (or refrained from using) the word 'monasticism'. Why, for instance, are certain movements labelled as 'monastic' while others with seemingly similar characteristics are not? For two illustrative examples, we may turn briefly to Judaism and Islam, religious traditions generally known for their rejection of monasticism as a religious and social option.

In ancient Judaism, there were groups such as the Essenes, described by Philo of Alexandria and other 1st-century CE writers as a community that fled the cities, lived without goods or property, shared things in common, were zealous for righteousness, obeyed a common rule, followed a daily regimen of prayer, wore simple clothing, restricted their diet, renounced the passions, and banned marriage. Some of the Essenes may have been associated with the community at Qumran, whose writings included the *Community Rule* and the other Dead Sea Scrolls. At that remote site in the Judean desert, the community dedicated themselves to a regime of ritual purity apart from the temple. But others seem to have remained in towns, and even married and had children. Philo also reports on another Jewish group called the Therapeutae, a mixed-gender community of ascetics that reputedly lived in the desert outside the city walls of Alexandria.

The Sufis of medieval Islam present a similar case in point. Sufism came to prominence as a contemplative movement in the 8th and 9th centuries, attracting Muslims interested in attaining mystical intimacy with God through ascetic training and introspection. Many Sufi masters and disciples lived in 'lodges' (Arabic *zāwiyah*, plural *zāwāyā*), which were sometimes equipped with libraries for study and hospices for care of the sick, not unlike medieval Western monasteries.

But despite certain social similarities, scholars have typically refrained from describing such Jewish and Islamic groups as 'monastic' in character. Why? Probably because the rabbis and Muslim leaders who have historically defined 'normative' Judaism and Islam discouraged the comparison. Thus, in interpreting the story of Adam and Eve in Genesis, the rabbinic author(s) of *Genesis Rabbah* declared that 'he who has no wife dwells without good, without help, without joy, without blessing, and without atonement'. For their part, Muslim commentators could point to the Qur'ān, where the divine voice says, 'Monasticism they [i.e. Christians] invented: we did not ordain it for them.' Or they could cite a saying (*ḥadīth*) attributed to Muhammad the Prophet: 'There is no monasticism in Islam.' As a result, Western scholars have tended to avoid this language in speaking about ascetic movements in Judaism and Islam.

Thus, notwithstanding the definitional questions posed by ancient Jewish sectarian communities and by medieval Sufism, 'monasticism' has traditionally been understood as a phenomenon primarily associated with Buddhism (and Jainism) in the

East and Christianity in the West. Accordingly, these traditions will receive the bulk of my attention. But I will also seek to tease out some of these definitional ambiguities further at different points, especially when I discuss monasticism in the modern world. In doing so, I will employ a variety of methods and approaches—including those related to sociology, gender studies, literature, art, theology, and archaeology—to highlight and assess what constitutes 'monastic' practices and communities across different periods, geographies, and religious traditions. In any case, the asking of such definitional questions has its own intrinsic value: it exposes our own unexamined assumptions about what it means to be a monk or nun, and it gives us eyes to recognize the diverse—and sometimes contradictory—forms of practice that we have commonly come to call 'monasticism' across disparate cultures and histories.

Chapter 2
Differences

In this chapter, I seek to outline a new approach to the question of how to engage responsibly in a comparative study of monasticism as a historical and cultural phenomenon found in multiple and varied forms. Another way to put this is that I want to give adequate account of the different 'monasticisms' (plural) that we encounter in our world. How are we able to assign this same label convincingly to a variegated field of monastic practices and communities that sometimes seem to stand in tension with each other? What models do we have at our disposal as we try to balance our need for definitions and the day-to-day differences that seem to resist any easy definition?

As a way to think through these questions, I will be drawing on the work of the late anthropologist Catherine Bell, whose research in the field of ritual studies has given us resources to think about how various kinds of monastic practices are themselves marked as acts of cultural 'differentiation'. In addressing the problem of how to define ritual, Bell focuses on the social process of what she calls 'ritualization'. In her book *Ritual Theory, Ritual Practice*, she defines it as follows:

> [Ritualization is] a way of acting that is designed and orchestrated to distinguish and privilege what is being done in comparison to other, usually more quotidian [i.e. everyday] activities...[a way of

acting that involves] specific strategies for setting some activities off from others, for creating and privileging a qualitative distinction between the 'sacred' and the 'profane'.

In short, for Bell, 'ritualization' involves a kind of strategic play. In and through certain structured bodily actions, ritual leaders and participants mark off their own practice as distinct from other modes of social activity.

In the process, participants shape the way that authority and power gets distributed within communities. In a typical Roman Catholic Mass, for example, the priests' intercessory authority and the congregation's subordination to God is 'ritualized' through bodily postures and through the layout of the space itself: the priest often stands in an elevated spot, raising his eyes to heaven, while the congregants kneel with heads bowed. As Bell puts it, '[K]neeling does not merely *communicate* subordination to the kneeler. For all intents and purposes, kneeling produces a subordinated kneeler in and through the act itself.'

How does this relate to the subject of monasticism? Let me begin on the level of generic description and then move to a more specific level. First, insofar as the daily lives of monastic communities are typically structured through ritual practices, we should expect them to participate in the differentiating dynamics characteristic of Bell's concept of 'ritualization'. In other words, as a species (or subset) of ritualizing practice, monasticism naturally engages in strategic acts of differentiation. Second, and even more importantly, however, we need to ask what is distinctive about monasticism as a venue for 'ritualization'. How do monastic communities engage in acts of differentiation in specific ways? This question, I think, will help put some meat on the bones of our definitional quest to figure out what different 'monasticisms' have in common.

Here, I want to think about monasticism(s) in terms of two unifying pairs of themes: (1) withdrawal and renunciation (as forms of spatial and bodily differentiation); and (2) regimentation and routinization (as forms of social differentiation).

As we shall see, in each of these areas, monastics have traditionally marked their own activities over against other more readily available social options. These forms of ritualization provide a means for re-enculturation to a markedly different(iated) lifestyle and worldview.

Withdrawal and renunciation

The life of a monk or a nun typically begins with a decision to *withdraw* from everyday society, to live a life spatially set apart. Closely linked with spatial separation are acts of *renunciation* such as poverty, fasting, and celibacy, which further serve to set monastics apart from the economic, dietary, and sexual mores of conventional households and civic society.

The earliest documented ascetics are attested in the *Upaniṣads*, a collection of authoritative Vedic Sanskrit texts that trace their origins to the 7th or 6th century BCE, but that underwent a process of later redaction into the Common Era. These early ascetics were what we might call proto-monastics—solitary, itinerant figures in northern India who decided to leave their natal homes and dwell in forests, subsisting by wandering and begging for food. The most common Sanskrit term for such figures was *sannyāsin*, 'one who gives up, abandons, renounces', but they were also called by the name *bhikṣu*, 'one who begs, asks for alms'.

Accordingly, the *Upaniṣads* emphasize how such ascetics 'gave up the desire for sons, the desire for wealth, and the desire for worlds, and undertook the mendicant life'. Elsewhere, the text lauds 'those in the wilderness, calm and wise, who live a life of penance and faith, as they beg their food'. As Patrick Olivelle notes in his commentary on this text, 'The householder is replaced by the celibate ascetic as the new religious ideal.' The withdrawal of such individuals from society—as well as their rejection of sex, family ties, and conventions of food and work—marked their distinct identity as forest dwellers and hermits. At the same time, far removed from the centres of Indian society, small-scale 'institutional' forms began to develop in these forest districts, with ascetic groups of followers and students congregating around charismatic teachers. Here, withdrawal, renunciation (*sannyāsa*), and discipleship were intimately linked.

In the 6th and 5th centuries BCE, the rise of Buddhist and Jain monastic movements emerged out of this same social milieu. Indeed, in the literature produced by both of these communities, the Pāli word for monk (*bhikkhu*) derives from the same root as the Sanskrit word for the type of wandering ascetic (*bhikṣu*) found in the *Upaniṣads*.

The Buddha's own life story is illustrative of this established pattern of Indian asceticism. After leaving home and family to wander in search of ascetic mentors, he eventually attained enlightenment and then attracted a cadre of disciples, who are thought to have formed the earliest Buddhist monastic community. That community was initially characterized by itinerancy, with only temporary settlements established at forest refuges during the rainy seasons. Over time, however, through gifts of buildings and property made by lay donors, Buddhist monastic communities evolved to embrace more sedentary patterns of residential and ritual life, even as solitary forest dwellers remained respected and revered figures.

Vardhamana Mahāvāra, a slightly older contemporary of the Buddha, is celebrated as a key early institutional founder of Jainism and as the last in a line of twenty-four illustrious divine teachers called *tirthankaras*—'ford-makers', i.e. those who create the *tirtha* (community) and are able to ford successfully across the waters of endless births and deaths on behalf of themselves and others. As in the case of the Buddha, the chronology of Mahāvāra's life has been debated, but the current scholarly consensus holds that he died c.425 BCE, only fifteen years or so before the Buddha's death. Like the Buddha, Mahāvāra left his family to wander the Ganges basin in northern India, seeking out the counsel of other independent ascetics, and concentrating his energies on fasting and meditating until he achieved enlightenment. Before his death he gathered to himself eleven brahman followers, who became heads of the Jain monastic order. Our earliest sources of knowledge for these scant biographical details are the *Acaranga* and *Sutrakritanga*, two books dated to the 3rd or 2nd century BCE and later incorporated in the Svetambara Jain scriptural canon.

One section of the *Acaranga* (1.9) emphasizes not only Mahāvāra's withdrawal from society, but also the harshness of his renunciatory practices, including his rejection of clothing, bathing, shelter, food, sleep, and human contact—austerities by which he sought to break the chains of body and mind, to separate the nascent monastic life from the world's cycles of birth and death, and thus to achieve enlightenment. Later Jain monks and nuns have sought to emulate Mahāvāra's status as a renouncer or 'striver' (*śramaṇa*)—a term and a corresponding set of bodily regimens that served to differentiate him from the brahmans, previously the only authorized social status for priestly or ascetic performance.

In this sense, both Jain and Buddhist monasticism constituted a critique of the Indian caste system and orthodox cults of sacrifice, replacing them with an emphasis on detachment from society and practices of renunciation, including a commitment to non-violence, lack of possessions, fasting, and celibacy. In this way, monastic communities—in and through their ritualized strategies of social differentiation—have sometimes played a crucial role in religious critiques of class structures (although at other times they have fallen prey to such critiques).

As competing monastic movements in north-eastern India, Jain and Buddhist communities also made marked efforts to distinguish their own ritual practice from each other's. While the Buddhist 'Middle Way' sought to chart an ascetic course between the extremes of self-indulgence and self-mortification, Jain renunciation took a more rigorous form, with Jain monks instructed to reside 'in a burial place or cremation ground, in a deserted house, below a tree, in solitude,…where no women live'. Jain nuns were likewise charged to live a homeless life of self-denial and to avoid places inhabited by men.

Jain and Buddhist monks came to wear different colour robes and adopted different policies with regard to carrying alms bowls. Jain monks either went naked or wore undyed robes and carried bowls made of gourd or wood. Buddhist monks donned red robes but were only allowed to use wooden bowls. Thus, in their ritualized acts of withdrawal and renunciation, Jain and Buddhist monastic communities not only differentiated themselves from non-ascetic lifestyle models (e.g. household and family, participation in civic governance), but also from other, alternative ascetic options in the social and religious marketplace of the Ganges River basin.

In the Mediterranean world, early Christian monasticism was also characterized by ritualized acts of withdrawal and renunciation. As mentioned earlier, the oldest documented form of Christian monasticism seems to have been that of individuals or of small, loosely-knit groups living in village or urban neighbourhood environments. This evidence, which only came to light in the 20th century through papyrological discoveries, contradicts the long-held, traditional image of the first Christian solitaries as isolated figures living a life of retreat in the desert, an image shaped by iconic tales like that of St Anthony, who is remembered for his successive stages of flight into the Egyptian hinterlands beyond the Nile Valley.

On this subject, two points are important to highlight. First, the decision by certain late Roman Egyptians and Syrians to set themselves apart within town settlements was itself a form of physical withdrawal and social renunciation, a departure from the centres of power and associated mores of civic society. Second, a close reading of St Anthony's famous *Life* actually gives us glimpses of how the earliest Christian monastics negotiated a subtle (and sometimes precarious) balance between isolation and self-deprivation on the one hand, and social contact on the other.

Probably written by the 4th-century bishop Athanasius of Alexandria, the *Life of Anthony* was meant to propagandize this new monastic movement as a valid expression of Christian spirituality. The plot of Anthony's *Life* takes him away from his family and his village, further and further into the outback of the Egyptian desert. But this movement happened in stages, and as such the story dramatizes a range of spatial locations for aspiring renunciants.

At the beginning of the story, Anthony is inspired to make a break from society when he hears two passages from the Gospel of Matthew (19:21 and 6:34) read in church. In response, he leaves his sister with some local ascetic women and 'devote[s] himself from then on to the discipline rather than the household'. Choosing as his mentor an old man in a neighbouring village 'who had practised from his youth the solitary life', Anthony begins by taking up residence 'in places proximate to his village' (*Life* 3). Already, we see several key assumptions at work for the 4th-century author: that he was familiar with groups of female 'virgins' living in village-based communities; that both Anthony and his unnamed older mentor initially pursued the monastic life within or near town settlements; and that their decision to live a solitary life nonetheless frequently involved loose social contracts between mentors and disciples. These details give us a varied sense of what a life of 'withdrawal' looked like for the earliest Christian monastics.

Later in Anthony's biography, he ventures out from his village and takes up residence in increasingly remote locations. First, he spends twenty years in an enclosed tomb 'situated some distance from the village' where friends would occasionally stop by 'to supply him periodically with bread' (*Life* 8). Next, he moves to a 'deserted fortress' on the outskirts of the irrigated land, at the foot of the 'mountain' (or cliffside) bordering the Nile Valley (*Life* 12). Finally, he relocates to a 'high hill' on the 'inner mountain', the desert plateau that extends for miles above the cliffside (*Life* 49 and 51). Today, his 'inner mountain' cell is commemorated as a cave located about thirty kilometres from the Red Sea. At each of these locations, he is eventually joined by larger and larger groups of followers, who take up residence in his vicinity and seek to emulate his example. Notably, in each successive stage, Anthony's withdrawal is framed as an act of differentiation: each spatial location of his monastic practice is differentiated not only from his town of origin but also from his previous ascetic abodes. In the story, his desire for solitude is continually held in tension with his own social role as mentor to other would-be monks.

In the *Life*, we are also told that Anthony endured a series of temptations by the devil, which serve to mark the stark terms of his renunciations. First, he was plagued by 'memories of his possessions, the guardianship of his sister, the bonds of kinship, love of money and of glory, the manifold pleasure of food, [and] the relaxations of life' (*Life* 4). Second, the devil appeared to Anthony at night 'in the form of a woman' and 'in the visage of a black boy' (*Life* 5–6), each representing the threat of 'fornication' for ancient monks trying to dissociate themselves from sexual desire. Third, Anthony experienced severe bodily pains associated with his stringent self-denial: these took the form of whippings and beatings administered by the demons, and as attacks in the night by wild beasts—'lions, bears, leopards, bulls, and serpents, asps, scorpions and wolves' (*Life* 8–9). Fourth and finally, he was accosted by visions of 'actual gold thrown in his path', a tangible sign of his struggle to separate himself from the dominant marketplace values of the late Roman world and to opt for an alternative economy of the spirit.

One observes a similar pattern in the *Life* of the early 5th-century Syrian monk, Simeon Stylites. In Simeon's case, he began by joining a community of monks before striking off on his own to engage in increasingly dramatic acts of withdrawal and renunciation. Over the course of his ascetic career, he bricked himself up in a hut for three years, he chained himself to a rock on top of a hill for five, he lived at the bottom of a well or cistern, and then began living on top of tall pillars (hence his name, Stylites, which comes the Greek word, *stylos*, meaning 'pillar'). The last thirty-six years of his life he spent on a 2.5-metre-square platform perched atop a 21-metre-tall pillar in northern Syria, the base of which still survives. All along, he pursued extreme practices of renunciation that would turn modern stomachs: he stood for so long the skin of his feet and belly burst open; his joints became dislocated from prostration; open sores became infected with maggots; his body reeked with a foul stench due to these ulcers and his refusal to bathe. For early Christian monks, such harsh forms of renunciation were not the norm, but in the story, his physical ailments and sufferings are meant to be visible signs of his separation from standard social expectations.

At the core of Simeon's and Anthony's *Lives*—and in the biographies of other Christian monks who followed in their wake—lies an irony that speaks to the fruits of such strategies of social differentiation. Even as Anthony tried to withdraw to ever more remote locations, he remained embedded in social networks that sustained his practice, first as a disciple to an older monastic mentor, and later as mentor himself to groups of devotees and followers. In the case of Simeon, even as he physically removed himself to the top of a 21-metre-tall pillar and engaged in forms of self-abnegation that made him repellent to both sight and smell, he attracted hundreds of international pilgrims who desired to see and (if possible) touch him, and his pillar became the physical centre of a large monastery housing scores of monks. While Simeon's extreme asceticism is most certainly a historical outlier, in the centuries since, monastic men and women have wrestled with a similar set of tensions—between withdrawal and forms of community; between the goal of renunciation and the implicit value given to bodily disciplines along the pathway to virtue.

Regimentation and routinization

Around the same time that solitaries like Anthony and Simeon were being celebrated as idealized models of the ascetic life, there is also evidence for the rise of monastic communities in which the values of withdrawal and renunciation were tempered and rechannelled. The early 20th-century sociologist Max Weber (1864–1920) would have described Anthony and Simeon as figures who embodied a kind of 'charismatic authority', founded on individual prowess and (inter)personal magnetism. But Weber also recognized the way that such *charisma* was 'routinized'—made stable, regular, and routine—through the rise of institutional structures. For such hermit heroes, 'routinizing' patterns could take forms as simple as the daily delivery of bread to one's cell, or mentor–disciple arrangements for transmitting monastic teachings. Or it could take more elaborate and translocal forms such as the organization of monastic federations, schools, and orders—networks of monasteries bound together by weekly worship or common rule.

In the 4th century and following, different kinds of organized and semi-organized Christian monastic communities developed in which charismatic and institutional forms of authority coexisted and were contested. One kind of (semi-organized) monastic settlement was the *lavra* type, which grew out of the aforementioned mentor–disciple arrangements. *Lavras* were loosely structured groups of hermits, each often accompanied by one or two younger monks, living in a cluster of mud-brick cells or caves, usually near a centrally located church where the community would gather on a weekly or occasional basis. The earliest documented *lavra*-type settlements were founded in the 4th and 5th centuries at Nitria and Scetis in northern Egypt and on the Judean desert plateau in Palestine.

Another (more highly organized) kind of monastic settlement was the cenobitic type. Cenobitic ('community-based') monasteries were usually heavily regimented through their defined hierarchy of leadership and a mandated adherence to a common rule. The classical example is the federation of monasteries founded in the 4th century by Pachomius in southern Egypt, and as a result this type of community is sometimes referred to as 'Pachomian monasticism'.

What was most distinctive about Pachomius' monastery was its governance by a system of rules. These rules set standards for entrance requirements, material possessions, manual labour, and a regimented daily schedule of work and prayer. The monasteries under Pachomius' authority were organized according to different jurisdictions and spaces: the monastics had their own cells, but they each also belonged to different houses within the monastery, and these houses were overseen by heads of houses who reported up a chain of command to Pachomius himself. Pachomius also introduced larger systemic innovations: pairs of monasteries for men and women, and a regional federation of at least eleven monasteries that shared the same schedule and were guided by the same rule. This elaborate organizational system inculcated an ethos of 'sameness' within the community, but it also provided the means by which Pachomian monks and nuns strategically differentiated themselves—from the society-at-large, from other non-rule-based monastic practitioners, and occasionally (in moments of ritualized disobedience) even from their cenobitic monastic compatriots.

Following Pachomius, the cenobitic system became the characteristic form of Christian communal monastic life in the West. Its enormous impact can be measured not only by cultivation of spiritual disciplines, but also by the larger cultural contributions of monasteries, which came to serve as centres for the production and preservation of books and as places specializing in the care of the sick. Monastic scriptoria and libraries played a foundational role for the development of medieval and modern universities (the architectural plans of the colleges at Oxford and Cambridge are modelled after cloisters), and monastic infirmaries played an equally instrumental role for the development of hospitals.

The impact of Pachomius' monastic foundation can also be measured in the rapid and diverse proliferation of similar communities across the late ancient Mediterranean and medieval European landscape. Later systems of rules—and the various reforms they embodied—show how the monastic life continued to be routinized and regimented, even as different monastic movements sought to distinguish themselves from one another through their careful recalibrations of ritual practice.

In Egypt, in fact, we know of at least one other monastic federation that derived its rules system from that of Pachomius. I am referring to the White Monastery Federation, a group of three monasteries (two for men and one for women) located across the Nile to the west, just downriver from Pachomius' headquarters. For an incredible eight decades this federation was headed by the irrepressible monk, Shenoute of Atripe (c.347–465 CE), who also has the distinction of being the most prolific author in the history of the Coptic language. His extensive writings include a collection of *Canons* that contain traces of his community's corpus of rules, a set of statutes that he enforced with an iron fist. I will have more to say about both Pachomius and Shenoute in Chapter 3.

But cenobitic monasticism, with its characteristic rule-based system, was certainly not restricted to Egypt. The 4th and 5th centuries witnessed the establishment of monastic communities associated with Basil of Caesarea in Asia Minor, Augustine of Hippo in North Africa, and John Cassian in Gaul. In each case, rules collections associated with these founding figures survive and give us a tangible sense of the way that such rules were adapted to other geographic and communal contexts. The Rules of St Basil, in particular, proved influential over the governance of monasteries in the Byzantine world. Theodore of Stoudios (760–826) adapted Basil's rule in founding his reformist Stoudite monastery in Constantinople, and his rule in turn ended up serving as the basis for 'The Rule of the Holy Mountain' implemented in the 10th and 11th centuries at Mount Athos (Hagion Oros) in north-eastern Greece.

In the West, the most well-known and influential of these early Christian monastic rules was the *Rule of St Benedict*, written in 6th-century Italy. Its stated purpose, as articulated by its author Benedict of Nursia (*c*.480–543/7), was 'to open a school for God's service, in which we hope nothing harsh or oppressive will be directed'. In such a statement, we see hints of routinization at work. By trying to avoid or moderate certain harsher ascetic practices, Benedict was seeking to distinguish his system from earlier, competing models. That is to say, he was founding his own 'school', where the primary ritualized curriculum was 'the work of God' (*opus Dei*)—a protocol of worship that served to punctuate both the day and the night with designated hours of prayer and 'sacred reading' (*lectio divina*).

Benedict's 'school' proved to be extraordinarily successful. Originally instituted at Monte Cassino south of Rome, his rule quickly became the prevailing model and guide for cenobitic monasticism throughout early medieval Europe. In the 7th and 8th centuries, use of Benedict's *Rule* spread to France, England, and Germany. In the early 9th century, his namesake, Benedict of Aniane, was appointed arch-abbot of all the monasteries in the territories ruled by the Emperor Charlemagne. This latter-day Benedict compiled the *Codex Regularum*, a compendium of rules incorporating and highlighting the original *Rules of St Benedict* but mandating somewhat stricter standards of behaviour (yet another subtle gesture of ritualized differentiation). But it was in the 11th century that the Benedictine movement reached its pinnacle at Cluny and its 'daughter houses' in eastern France. The reforms instituted at Cluny de-emphasized the importance of manual labour for monks. Instead, such labour was assigned to an expanded cadre of servants, and the monks dedicated themselves primarily to the precise details of liturgical performance. In this context, the Divine Office (*officium divinum*) at Cluny became grander and more elaborate, with the use of golden vessels and utensils, the addition of extra hymns and songs to the Virgin and the angels, and increased attention to the veneration of the saints and their relics.

Over time, the medieval European landscape became populated with a variety of different monastic 'orders', each with its own ritualized sense of identity and practice. The Cistercian order, founded in 1098 at Cîteaux, France, represented a direct (and rather sober) reaction to the liturgical exuberance of Cluny. Cistercian monks returned to an emphasis on manual labour and to an unadorned office of prayer based on a more literal adherence to Benedict's *Rule*.

At the same time, other reform movements developed their own rule systems with distinct points of emphasis. In the late 11th century, in the foothills of the French Alps, Carthusian monks sought a return to the hermit ideal. The monastery they founded, Grande Chartreuse, was constructed as a collection of stone cells around a central cloister: its physical layout and sparer liturgy were meant to allow room for solitude, private prayer, and the reading and copying of books. In this way, the Carthusian community explicitly constructed a rule that integrated aspects of solitary and cenobitic life.

At the same time, the 11th, 12th, and 13th centuries also saw the rise of other rules and orders that exhibited a more tenuous and complicated relationship to 'monastic' identity. One such rule was the *Rule of St Augustine* (an 11th-century document not in fact composed by the saint himself), which was more broadly framed than Benedict's *Rule*. It emphasized poverty, simplicity, and good works modelled more on the example of the apostles than that of the desert fathers. Followers of the *Rule* were technically called 'canons' or 'canonesses'—not monks or nuns—and fell into two general categories: 'canons regular' (who dedicated themselves to pastoral care); and 'friars' (who dedicated themselves to a mendicant life of poverty). To make matters more complicated, there were also lay Augustinians who did not take vows. In the 11th and 12th centuries, the Augustinian order quickly spread throughout Europe—Italy, France, Spain, Germany, Austria, and the British Isles—offering an alternative way of life to that of the Benedictines.

Finally, the 12th century witnessed the rise of two more orders that similarly avoided use of the title 'monk'. These were the Dominicans and the Franciscans, whose founders—Dominic (*c.*1172–1221) and Francis of Assisi (1181–1226)—were contemporaries of each other. Both established communities of friars and nuns who were peripatetic in lifestyle (that is, not bound to a specific home abbey). Dominic and his canon-followers adopted the *Rule of St Augustine* and applied themselves to the missionary vocation of preaching. Francis drafted his own rule—the *Rule of St Francis*—which committed his followers to a mendicant life of serving the poor. As was the case for the Augustinian order, Dominic and Francis stamped their communities with distinct kinds of quasi-monastic (or counter-monastic) identity.

In these examples, we encounter once again a complex terrain in the Western monastic social landscape and the blurred lines that sometimes exist between monastic and non-monastic self-definition. I have been describing how a diversity of rule-based movements and orders proliferated in the late ancient Mediterranean and medieval Europe, and I have analysed them in terms of what

Catherine Bell described as 'ritualization'—the privileging of certain sets of practices over against others and the resulting production of differentiated ascetic lifestyles. A similar model may be applied in studying the rise of various rule-based Jain and Buddhist 'monasticisms' in South, South-East, and East Asia.

Both Jain and Buddhist monasticism developed sets of rules for the regulation of community practices. Indeed, these rules took shape in conjunction with different kinds of monastic groupings. As mentioned earlier, from their early roots in ancient India, Jain and Buddhist monks distinguished themselves from each other through the colour of their robes and the kind of alms bowls they carried—distinctions legislated in their respective rules corpora. But they also exhibited internal differentiations, as monastic sects or movements arose within each community and as Buddhism spread outside of India and began to adapt to new cultural contexts in South-East Asia, Tibet and Mongolia, China, Korea, and Japan.

Throughout its history, up to the present, Jain monasticism has remained predominantly within an Indian geographical orbit. But even within its subcontinent of origin, Jain practice has taken different regimented forms. There are two monastic orders that dominate the Jain religious landscape in India: the Svetambara and Digambara movements. Both adhere to sets of rules that authorize—and routinize—a lifestyle of wandering, homeless begging, often practised by small groups of mendicant ascetics. Even as settled monastic institutions developed, the itinerant life remained an ideal. As part of their vows, both commit themselves not to harm any other form of life.

But there are subtle (and not-so-subtle) differences as well. Monks and nuns belonging to the Svetambara movement follow a code of conduct that allows them to wear white robes and to carry a woollen bed sheet, a woollen mat, and a broom made with woollen threads to brush away any insects on which they might

1. Manuscript illumination showing Digambara monks walking in a forest carrying water pots and peacock-feather brooms. Ink on silk, probably 15th century CE.

unwittingly sit or tread during their travels. The Digambara sect forbids monks from wearing any clothes (although a dispensation for clothing is made in the case of nuns), and only authorizes them to carry a broom made of peacock feathers and a water gourd (see Figure 1).

These differences between monastics in the Digambara and Svetambara traditions originally emerged out of an early schism in the Jain community based in part on different attitudes towards nakedness as a sign of renunciation and on different views of their authoritative scriptures. Over time, the rejection of clothing within male Digambara circles became regimented practice. This ethic was reinforced through the visual depiction of the founder Mahāvāra and later Jain saints as nude figures: in one prominent example, a 10th-century CE statue of the saint Bahubali erected on a high outcropping of rock in Karnataka (south-western India) can be seen from thirty kilometres away and has been the object of a longstanding pilgrimage practice. By contrast, Svetambara monks have a more equivocal attitude towards nudity. Accordingly, they have established two paths for practitioners: the *jinakalpa* (where monks eschew clothing) and the *sthavirakalpa* (where monks don white robes). Nuns in both movements remain clothed.

One observes parallel but distinctive processes of regimentation and routinization for ancient and medieval Buddhist monastic communities. Alongside solitary and itinerant forms of ascetic practice, settled communities or monasteries developed in India, regulated by sets of rules and punctuated by ritual observances. Three such observances are the biweekly *Poshadha* ceremony, when the community gathers, recites the rules, and marks days of fasting; the *Pravarana*, a rite in which monks invite others to point out wrongs for confession; and the *Kathina* ceremony, which marks the end of the three-month rainy season retreat and provides an opportunity for donations of new robes and the temporary relaxation of certain precepts.

As monastic canons and rules corpora were adapted for use, different branches or 'schools' of Buddhism developed, the best known of which today are Theravāda, Mahāyāna, and Vajrayāna. Each of these schools has its own emphases, but there is also considerable overlap in practice. These are not monastic schools, but they serve as the broader religious landscape in which Buddhist monastic communities have developed.

Theravāda Buddhism, which probably traces its roots to the late centuries BCE, relies on the Pāli Canon and stresses the importance of self-reliance, direct personal experience, and the path of the *arhat*—one who is worthy or perfected—as the route to awakening. Attaining full Buddhahood is reserved for only a select few. While Theravāda originated in India, it became the dominant form of Buddhist practice in Sri Lanka and later in South-East Asia.

Mahāyāna Buddhism, which differentiated itself in the early centuries CE, envisions the pathway to enlightenment as a process of moving beyond the status of *arhat* to the *bodhisattva* ideal of attaining the compassion of the Buddha. Today, Mahāyāna is the most widespread and populous school of practice, having spread from India to China, Korea, Japan, Tibet and Mongolia, and parts of South-East Asia.

Vajrayāna Buddhism, also known as Tantric Buddhism, emerged in the early medieval period (c.6th–8th centuries CE), featuring a pronounced emphasis on forms of esoteric meditation involving the recitation of spells and (at an advanced stage) the visualization of deities. Also known as Tantric Buddhism or the 'Thunderbolt Vehicle', Vajrayāna is most closely associated with Tibet, but it also played a role in the development of Buddhist practice in Sri Lanka, Indonesia, South-East Asia, China, Korea, Japan, and Mongolia.

As Buddhist monasticism spread beyond the borders of India, it was shaped not only by these broader schools of practice but also by local and regional processes of enculturation. Theravāda Buddhism was introduced to Sri Lanka during the reign of King Dēvānāmpiyatissa (c.250–210 BCE). In the capital city of Anurādhapura, three major monasteries were established from the 3rd century BCE to the 3rd century CE. One of these monasteries (Mahāvihāra) promoted literal adherence to the Pāli Canon. The other two (Abhayagiri and Jētavana) were more flexible in the application of the Canon, and more open to 'foreign influences, including Mahāyāna ideas and Tantric popular practices', an openness confirmed by recent archaeological excavations. During the 12th-century reign of King Parākramabāhu I (1153–1186), all three monasteries came under Mahāvihāra control and other traditions were suppressed. Sri Lankan monks played an instrumental role in bringing Theravāda Buddhism to South-East Asia. Indeed, their version of the Pāli Canon and their voluminous commentaries on it served as vehicles for the conversion of village populations throughout the kingdoms of Burma, Thailand, Laos, and Cambodia.

In late antiquity, Mahāyāna Buddhism was brought to China either by land or by sea in conjunction with Silk Road trading routes, and monastics played a crucial role in its missionary propagation and in the translation of scriptural texts into Chinese. With its characteristic emphasis on withdrawal, Buddhist monasticism ran counter to certain highly prized societal values in China (especially the Confucianist emphasis on a this-worldly, humanistic code of ethics), but the movement gradually gained a foothold, in part because its emphasis on meditation was interpreted as compatible with Daoist teachings. In turn, Buddhist practices came to influence the rise of Daoist monasticism in the 6th century, including rules corpora and the configuration of monastic architecture.

By the 6th, 7th, and 8th centuries, multiple schools of Buddhist monastic practice had emerged in China. These included Pure Land, Three Stages, Tiantai, Sanlun, Lu, Faxiang, Huayan, Chan (Zen), and Zhenyan, with several of these schools establishing temples and monasteries in mountain territories (e.g. the Tiantai school at Mount Tiantai). In the middle of the 9th century (840–845 CE), the Tang Emperor Wuzong initiated a severe policy of suppression and persecution of Buddhist monasticism (as well as other religious communities viewed as 'foreign' to China), and as a result some of these Buddhist schools ceased to exist. The Pure Land and Chan schools survived, however, and became the predominant forms of Buddhist monasticism in the country. Pure Land Buddhism is characterized by its emphasis on 'rebirth' in a cosmological realm (Pure Land) governed by Amitābha Buddha. It is known for being open to laypersons as well as monks due to its more relaxed, informal, and less hierarchical system of practices. Chan Buddhism, by contrast, is known for its more rigorous disciplines of meditation practice and stricter adherence to the Vinaya code.

A similar pattern pertained in both Korea and Japan. Buddhist monasticism was likewise introduced to these areas by travelling monks, underwent a process of cultural assimilation, and developed into multiple schools of thought and practice. In Korea,

Buddhism was brought into dialogue with indigenous forms of shamanistic folk religiosities, while in Japan it came into intersection with Shintoism, which placed a strong emphasis on the instrumental efficacy of ritual acts. In both areas, the proliferation of monastic schools bore a strong relation to Chinese precedents. Thus, for example, in Korea, the Kyeyul and Pŏpsang schools were founded in the 7th century CE by Chinese monks who based their teachings on the Lu and Faxiang curricula mentioned earlier. Pure Land and Chan (Sŏn) movements also proliferated, with the latter becoming the most prevalent. The largest Sŏn denomination is the Jogye (Chogye) order, which oversees 840 temples, ninety meditation monasteries, and approximately ten million adherents, of which around 10,000 are monastics.

In Japan, the 7th, 8th, and 9th centuries also witnessed the rise of multiple schools (e.g. Jōjitsu, Sanron, Hossō, Kusha, Kegon, and Ritsu), including certain esoteric and tantric sects (e.g. Shingon and Tendai). During the medieval period, other kinds of monastics also populated the Japanese landscape. These ranged from itinerant monks who engaged in a kind of perpetual pilgrimage, to mountain ascetics who lived in treacherous places at high altitudes, to mendicants who begged for subsistence from house to house, to an ascetic sect called Fuke whose members (called Komusō) walked the streets blowing flutes (*shakuhachi*) with baskets over their heads, a gesture meant to mark the absence of ego (see Figure 2).

Not all of these schools and practices survived, but as was the case in Korea the importation of Pure Land and Chan (Zen) practices proved to be extremely influential. Indeed, by the early 13th century, Chan (Zen) Buddhism in Japan had taken deep root, established as an independent religious order with multiple branches (e.g. Rinzai, Sōtō, and Ōbaku), all derived from Chinese traditions. Today, it is the most recognizable form of Japanese Buddhism not only in East Asia but also as a cultural and religious export in the West.

2. Print of a Komusō monk in the Fuke school begging for alms from a courtesan and her attendant. Isoda Koryūsai (1735–90), *Courtesan and Her Attendant Use Mirrors to Identify a Komusō*.

Buddhist monasticism may have taken root in Tibet as early as the 8th century CE. Medieval chronicles credit the establishment of the first Tibetan monastery at Samye to King Trisong Detsen (*c.*740–798), who is said to have founded it with the help of an Indian monk-scholar named Santiraksita and a practitioner of yoga meditation (yogin) named Padmasambhava. In this account, the foundation of the Samye monastery is associated with two important streams of Tibetan practice: intellectual scholasticism and esoteric prowess. But it would not be until the 12th and 13th century that formalized monastic schools developed, each with its own distinctive emphasis.

Four main schools or orders (*chölug*) came to dominate the medieval and early modern Buddhist landscape in Tibet. All have suborders with flagship monastic institutions that function as training centres headed by senior lamas (teachers) who embody particular teaching lineages.

The two earliest Tibetan monastic schools were the Sakyapa in western Tibet and the Kagyüpa, in central Tibet. The latter traces its teaching lineage to the early disciples of the famous Tibetan saint Milarepa (1043–1123), whose extraordinary life story we will revisit in Chapter 4.

Also based in central Tibet, a third school, the Gelukpa, emerged later in the 15th century but would go on to become the most populous and influential of the monastic orders. Indeed, the Dalai Lama—regarded as the successive incarnation of enlightened teachers—has served as the senior teaching figure in the Gelukpa order since 1546, and since 1642 has been regarded as the Tibetan head of state by his monastic followers.

Finally, the fourth school, Nyingmapa, began as a smaller-scale medieval teaching lineage similarly led by hereditary lamas, but it was later organized into a larger-scale monastic institution in the early modern period. A parallel pattern of development was followed by the Bon (P'önpo)—an indigenous Tibetan religious sect that likewise transitioned from a system of largely autonomous local lama leaders (called terpas or tertöns) to one dominated by monastic teaching foundations with more formalized programmes of training.

The primary distinction between these different Tibetan monastic schools lies in their relative emphasis on philosophical study versus esoteric tantra (Vajrayāna). The Gelukpa order stresses the importance of intensive training in Buddhist philosophy and debate—through a long and rigorous curriculum of study in monastic colleges—as foundational for any later advancement to tantric meditational and ritual practices. By contrast, the three other Buddhist orders (as well as the Bon sect) provide their monastic denizens with opportunities for earlier engagement with yogic tantra as an accelerated path to enlightenment.

In the proliferation of Buddhist monastic schools and movements from India to Sri Lanka, South-East Asia, China, Korea, Japan, and Tibet, we see once again processes of regimentation and routinization at work. Via practices of scriptural transmission and commentary, and through ritualized teaching lineages and curricula, different ways of being monastic emerged. As in the case of the ancient Mediterranean and medieval Europe, so too with Jainism and Buddhism (along with Daoism) in various parts of Asia: the result was a diversity of 'monasticisms'—a complex landscape of monastic communities that require careful study to understand their rules of living, their ideals and worldviews, and their physical spaces and everyday life. It is to these themes that I turn in Chapters 3–5.

Chapter 3
Rules, social organization, and gender

As noted previously, monastic communities take a variety of forms—from mentor–disciple pairs and small clusters of monastics living largely independent lives, to highly structured communal institutions regulated according to a common life and rule. In this chapter, I turn my attention to the social organization of community-based monasticism and to the function of rules for the shaping of monastic identity and practice. With this focus in mind, I present case studies from both Buddhist and Christian contexts. My study of Buddhist monastic codes draws on different versions of the *Vinaya* (originally introduced in Chapter 1), while my investigation of Christian monastic codes delves into two late ancient examples from Upper Egypt. These rule collections present very different challenges to the historian. We will use these sources to explore how monastic lifestyles and identities replaced conventional civic and familial models, and how gendered forms of monastic life were regulated and sometimes crucially differentiated from each other in practice.

Before we proceed, however, I want to introduce two helpful concepts for understanding how monastic rules function for monks and nuns who renounce 'the world' and commit themselves to following such precepts. The first is 'resocialization', a concept drawn from the sociology of knowledge. This term highlights the way a person who enters a monastery finds him or herself undergoing a

3. A boy has his head shaved by a Buddhist monk during an initiation ceremony called 'Children Becoming Buddhist Monks' at a Jogye (Sŏn) temple in Seoul, Korea.

process of radical reorientation. Bentley Layton has described this as a process of 'total world replacement' ritually mediated by a complex system of new rules to be internalized and enacted. This can involve not only shifts in location and institutional organization but also bodily alterations, including changes in dress, the removal or covering of one's hair, and even burn marks or tattoos on the skin (see Figure 3). In each context, rules and ritual practices typically serve as the primary mechanisms for shaping the texture of the monastic's new identity and social reality.

The second helpful concept is 'form-of-life', a term used by the philosopher Ludwig Wittgenstein to describe how humans use language to find agreement based on assumptions they take for granted and hold in common in the course of everyday communication. Recently, the concept has been adopted and developed by Giorgio Agamben in his study of medieval monastic rules. Agamben was interested in differentiating between the function of laws on the one hand, and the use of rules as a holistic way of life on the other. In this context, monastic rules 'are not truly laws or precepts in the strict sense of the term', but rather they 'declare and show to the monks the obligations they had agreed to, given the kind of life they had professed'. In other words, monastic rules are not external standards to be adhered to; but rather, in the context of a life shared in common, they are internalized, already-acknowledged ways of being in the world that replace previous sets of civic commitments. For monks and nuns living in organized, communal monasteries, rules thus come to embody a 'form-of-life'—that is, 'a life that is linked so closely to its form that it proves to be inseparable from it'. With this distinction between laws and rules in mind, let us turn to our case studies, beginning with processes of monastic initiation, and then continuing with the regulation of daily life, as stipulated in both Buddhist and Christian rules corpora. In each case, I will call special attention to gender formation and the way that monastic rules were employed to regulate monastic bodies and movements within communal settings.

How resocialization starts: Buddhist and Christian monastic rites of ordination/initiation

The process of resocialization, or world replacement, begins immediately upon entry into a monastery, when a person leaves behind the world outside its walls and dedicates him or herself to a new community and a new set of countercultural, ascetic standards. It should not be surprising, then, that this process of entry is choreographed with considerable care in both Buddhist and Christian settings.

The *Vinaya* of the *Mūlasarvāstivādin* school of Buddhist monasticism, originally transmitted in Sanskrit but later translated and preserved in Tibetan, details a rite of ordination for men who petition to become monks and join a *vihāra*, or monastic community. (There is no corresponding early account of female monastic ordination.) The male ordination rite was scripted as follows.

After the community gathers and makes confession for any offence committed over the past half month, the prospective monk does reverence before the Buddha and his teachers, prostrating himself and embracing them around their knees. He is then vested with his three monastic robes and given his eating bowl, which are each examined to determine their suitability and conformance to established standards. Finally, the candidate is asked a series of questions designed to verify his (male) gender identity, social standing, and health. The first round of questions is conducted by a certain 'Monk-Who-Instructs-the-Candidate-in-Private', who takes him aside and interviews him one-on-one. The second round of questions (virtually identical to the first) takes place within the designated communal ritual space and is conducted by the gathered community as a whole.

What do these initiatory questions tell us about the process of resocialization and the shaping of Buddhist monastic identity? First, the male gendering of the rite is explicit from the outset. The questioner begins by asking, 'Are you a man? Do you have a male organ?' And later, 'Not a eunuch? Not a hermaphrodite? Not a despoiler of nuns?...Have you fully practised the practice of chastity?' In this way, the ritual seeks to frame the monastic community, and the celibate bodies that inhabit it, as unambiguously male. As a result, from the start, the ritual inscribes a starkly binary boundary between monastery and world, between male and other. The category of 'other' includes not only women, eunuchs, and hermaphrodites, but also non-human entities. Thus, the candidate is also asked whether he is 'a magically created phantom' or 'an animal'. In each case, the expected answer is, 'I am not'.

The other questions asked of the candidate focus primarily on his social standing and health. Are his parents still living and do they authorize his petition to become a monk? Is he a slave, or a thief, or a royal officer, or a member of another religious community, or a murderer, or a debtor? Has he committed one of the four offences that lead to expulsion, i.e. violating one's vow of celibacy, stealing, taking a life, or lying about one's spiritual attainments? In posing these questions, the monastic community seeks to determine whether the candidate remains constrained by worldly ties and bonds, whether those ties be economic, political, social, or moral in character.

Finally, the candidate is interrogated about whether he suffers from illness, and here the rite provides a detailed list of medical conditions that afflicted the larger society but must be, at least ostensibly, excluded from the monastic corporate body:

> Venerable, you must hear! These various sorts of bodily illness arise in the body of men, namely leprosy, goitre, boils, exanthema, blotch, scabs, itch, carbuncle, psoriasis, consumption, epilepsy, Prader-Willi syndrome, jaundice, elephantiasis, scrotal hernia, fever, virulent fever, one-day fever, chronic fever, lethargy arising from fever, cutaneous eruption, spasmodic cholera, wheezing, cough, asthma, bloody abscess, rheumatism, swelling of the glands, blood disease, liver disease, haemorrhoids, vomiting, retention of the urine, fatigue, elevated body heat, burning in the chest and bone disease—do you not have some of these sorts of illness or others like them?

This comprehensive litany of illnesses (along with the list of questions about social ties) has a specific purpose: it draws a ritualized boundary between the outside and inside. By denying any association with illness and any external moral obligations, the candidate and the gathered community effectively mark the monastery as a place free from bodily impurities and societal constraints, as a place ritually distinguished from *saṃsāra*, the cycle of birth, death, and rebirth.

For a comparative case study, let us to turn to a pair of Christian monastic rules from late ancient Egypt: the *Rules* of Pachomius and Shenoute. The Pachomian *Rules* provide us with our earliest evidence for a Christian monastic community governed by a common rule. In the text, we get a fleeting glimpse of the process whereby prospective monks would have gained entry to one of Pachomius' monasteries. The Shenoutean *Rules* represent a slightly later collection based on a Pachomian model but belonging to a different federation of monasteries in Egypt.

According to the Pachomian *Rules*, when a prospective monk arrives at the gate of the monastery, the head of the monastery is first informed. Then the prospective monk undergoes a waiting period outside the gate, during which he endeavours to learn the Lord's Prayer, the Psalms, and perhaps other passages of Scripture. After this period of scriptural memorization, the candidate is asked a series of questions about his prior history and worldly ties: 'Has he done something wrong and, troubled by fear, suddenly run away? Or is he under someone's authority? Can he renounce his parents and spurn his own possessions?' These sample questions are not unlike some of those asked in the second phase of inquiry for prospective Buddhist monks as described in the *Vinaya*.

After this period of questioning, the person wanting to enter the monastery is given instructions in the rules of the community, and then he is stripped of his old clothes and given a monastic habit. Finally, the doorkeeper brings him before the rest of the brothers at the time of prayer, and he is told to sit in his assigned place.

The protocol followed in the Pachomian monasteries was picked up and adapted by the Egyptian communities under Shenoute's leadership. In the Shenoutean federation, when a person inquiring about becoming a monk arrived at the gate of the monastery he was similarly welcomed by the gatehouse worker. Then the 'father of the congregation' (Shenoute himself) was summoned to scrutinize the would-be monk in a test of his qualifications and to communicate the rules of the monastery, probably in abridged form. At this stage, the candidate was asked to renounce his possessions orally. Within three months' time—the official trial period for new monks—he would need to transfer his property legally in writing to the monastic federation. Finally, the head of the monastery would lead the person into the church where he would take an oath of obedience, be assigned to a specific congregation, strip himself of his old clothes and put on new monastic garb.

In these two examples from Upper Egypt, we observe how would-be monks underwent a process of initiation akin to a 'rite of passage', as theorized by Arnold van Gennep and later by Victor Turner. This process involves first a severing of previous social connections, a separation reinforced and confirmed through the process of questioning inquirers about their situation and motives. The second step is a transitional or liminal phase, during which the petitioner stands betwixt and between worlds, both physically and symbolically. In the Pachomian and Shenoutean communities, the designated space for this transition is the gatehouse, where the prospective monk begins to be resocialized through practices of scriptural memorization and instruction in the monastic rules. Third and finally comes a stage of incorporation or integration, whereby a new status is achieved. In the case of these Egyptian monasteries (again not unlike that of their Buddhist counterparts in India and Tibet) the incorporation of new monks into the community is effected through rites involving oaths of obedience, change of dress (the stripping away of worldly garb and the putting on of monastic vestments), and placement within the organizational and spatial hierarchy of the congregation, under the authority of their superior.

Early Buddhist monastic codes as form-of-life

Ordination ceremonies and rites of initiation only represent the very first step in a monastic's process of resocialization and world replacement. What follows are the daily, weekly, and yearly rhythms of life within a monastery, and these rhythms are typically established and maintained—often in minute detail—by adherence to a shared corpus of established rules and an underlying ethic of obedience to authority. I have noted that such sets of rules should not be thought of as 'laws', but rather (in Wittgenstein's and Agamben's language) as a 'form-of-life'—a communally cultivated and internalized way of being in the world. What did this look like in practice?

To get a sense of how such rules work, let us turn to another *Vinaya* tradition, the *Pātimokkha*, a corpus of rules preserved in Pāli that evolved over the course of several centuries, achieving its final form around the 1st century CE. This corpus would become a canonical component of Theravādin Buddhist monastic practice in subsequent centuries, especially in Sri Lanka and South-East Asia. In my analysis of this source, I will pay special attention to how its authors sought to regulate bodies and define gender boundaries within early Buddhist monastic foundations. As Gregory Schopen has noted, the rules in such *Vinaya*-literature were primarily prescriptive, not descriptive: they present an aspirational and idealized picture of the monastic life. But by examining their operating assumptions, we can learn quite a lot about the function of such rules in the shaping of Buddhist monastic identity.

In the *Bhikkhu Pātimokkha*—the Buddhist canon of rules for male Theravādin monks—monastic identity is crucially framed in terms of ritual practice and the regulation of male bodies. The preliminary duties of the monks include a set of prescribed actions meant to mark ritualized time and space as pure and thus suitable for proper recitation. The Pāli term for ritualized time is *uposatha*, and the ritualized space could be an assembly hall, a pavilion, or even the foot of a tree. The prescribed actions include sweeping with a broom, lighting a lamp, preparing water for drinking and washing, and arranging seats. The practice of recitation that follows involves first the revelation of offences by individual monks. To lie or dissemble about one's previous offences was considered an 'obstructing matter'—something that precluded the community's ritual purpose of purification. Finally, having disclosed all offences, the purified community recites the rules corpus in its entirety, a cognitive and corporeal act whereby the gathered monks remember and internalize their shared monastic values.

The contents of the *Bhikkhu Pātimokkha* consist of an eclectic mix of rules for policing the body (including its interaction with other bodies), with the goal of ensuring that the community remained pure in intent and in practice. The first four rules deal with major violations that 'entail defeat' and result in the expulsion of the monk from the monastery: sexual intercourse, theft, taking a life, and lying about one's own reputed supernatural powers. These first four are followed by thirteen more 'matters entailing a formal meeting' to determine the punitive consequences for a range of transgressive bodily and verbal actions, such as the emission of semen, bodily contact, and pimping on the one hand, and lewd words, sexual speech, and false accusations on the other. Two other 'indefinite rules' highlight certain specific contexts where monks might be susceptible to these temptations. Of special concern are occasions where they find themselves sitting on a seat with a female monastic: in such circumstances monks are warned about coming into physical contact or engaging in intimate speech with women.

The rules in the *Bhikkhu Pātimokkha* number 227 in total. In addition to the nineteen statutes outlined in the previous paragraph, there are another 126 matters entailing expiation or confession, plus eighty-two more requiring training or legal processes. Many of these again focus on the monastic body. More than twenty rules pertain to robes and proper standards of dress. More than thirty pertain to bowls and dietary restrictions. Others forbid monks from specific interactions with nuns: not just sharing a bed or a seat, but also teaching them while alone or at night, entering a nun's residence, exchanging goods, or going on a journey together. The rules even go so far as to micromanage matters of bodily decorum: monks are to keep their robes worn evenly all around and their eyes downcast. They are not to laugh or make a loud sound. They are not to let their bodies sway to and fro, swing their arms, shake their heads or their hands, stand or walk with arms akimbo, cover their heads, walk on their heels or toes, stuff their cheeks or speak with their mouth full, stick out their tongue, smack their lips or make a sucking sound, lick their hands or their bowl, or defecate while standing.

What would this hyper-detailed attention to bodily boundaries and decorum have produced in the male monastic communities that sought to adhere to these statutes? In his work *Being and Nothingness*, the philosopher Jean-Paul Sartre pauses to observe how a waiter in a café regulates his movements, gestures, and voice as part of a social performance of 'waiterliness': he 'plays with his condition in order to realize it'. In the same way, sociologist Erving Goffman has noted how status or social position is a product of behaviour, 'something that must be enacted and portrayed, something that must be realized' through bodily dispositions of etiquette, dress, deportment, deference, and demeanour. Something similar held true for early Buddhist monks in India: the *Bhikkhu Pātimokkha* served as the script for their performance of monastic identity. It was a performance that consisted of ritualized actions by the community gathered (sweeping, lighting lamps, preparing water, reciting rules) and the regimentation of bodily decorum for individual monks in their day-to-day lives. Central to this male monastic decorum was the maintenance of physical boundaries and separation from female bodies (monastic or otherwise).

When one examines the corresponding early collection of rules for Buddhist nuns—the *Bhikkhunī Pātimokkha*—one observes how concerns about gender differentiation and bodily purity also distinctively stamped the contours of the female monastic world. The rules for male monks were the product of a process of accretion as new statutes were added over time to address previously unanticipated situations in the life of Buddhist monasteries, and in this context the later rules for women may be seen as a further outgrowth and expansion upon that original corpus. Most of the rules in the *Bhikkhunī Pātimokkha* replicate the rules for men, but there are crucial additions. Indeed, the women's monastic code contains a total of 311 rules, eighty-four more than the men's monastic code, and these additions underscore at points the unequal status of female monastics, who are subject to even more rigorous scrutiny within the community.

Instead of four rules entailing defeat, for example, the nuns were required to recite and remember eight. They must refrain not only from sexual intercourse, theft, taking a life, and lying about one's own reputed supernatural powers, but also from making contact with a man 'above the circle of the knees', from concealing the fault of another nun, from following the teaching of a male monk who has been suspended, and from assorted other kinds of interactions with men, including holding hands, touching a cloak, engaging in conversation, or arranging a meeting. In other sections of the monastic code, the rules for women expand, and the cumulative effect is a more comprehensive system of surveillance and control over female bodies.

This is especially evident in a section of the *Bhikkhunī Pātimokkha* governing 166 'matters entailing expiation'. By contrast, the same section of the *Bhikkhu Pātimokkha* (the men's rules) contains only ninety-two such statutes. One of the things that stands out in a comparison of the two corpora is how extensively the rules police the nuns' physical separation from male monks as well as from non-ordained men. Thus, a nun should not enter a monastery or a park with monks in it without permission. She should not 'stand with drinking water or with a fan near a bhikkhu while he is eating'. Nor should she 'stand together with or…talk with one man, in the dark of night', 'in a screened place', 'in an open place', 'on a carriage road or in a cul-de-sac or at a crossroads'. The injunction against sitting with a man privately is important enough to repeat two more times later in the list of rules. But the monitoring of female bodies goes even further: nuns should not get close enough to 'whisper in [a man's] ear', nor should they become physically intimate enough to allow a 'boil or scab…on the lower half of her body' to 'be washed' by a man. Left unspoken in many of these statutes is the underlying danger of potential sexual contact. Such a concern surfaces at other points in the text, where it becomes explicit that a nun should not 'make her bed together with a man'.

Notably, this same concern also extends to same-sex familiarity with other women. The rules closely monitor the proximity of nuns' bodies from each other: they should not 'lie down on one couch' or 'lie down having one carpet and cover'. A nun should not knowingly make her bed too close to that of another nun, nor should she 'make her bed for more than two or three nights' with women who are not ordained. By the same token, a nun should not allow herself to be rubbed or massaged by another nun, by a monastic trainee, or by a female novice. None of these stipulations is applied to male monks as moral subjects in the corresponding section of the *Bhikkhu Pātimokkha*. The end result is that this canonical set of monastic rules creates parallel and yet crucially differentiated subjectivities for Buddhist monks and nuns in their bodily disposition and daily practice as renunciants.

These monastic subjectivities are shaped not simply by encounters with a written set of rules, but more fundamentally by periodic ritualized acts of reciting those rules and of putting them into daily practice. To use Nirmala Salgado's terminology, it is the 'renunciant everyday'—routine duties such as 'maintaining and running a hermitage, cooking, cleaning, meditating, accepting alms from supporters, counseling, performing religious services, and teaching'—that marks Buddhist communal life under a monastic rule. At the same time, the identities of monks and nuns are also inevitably shaped by small (and large) acts of resistance. At the end of this chapter I will discuss monks and nuns who break the rules, and how such forms of disobedience contribute to the shaping of monastic subjectivities. Before I get there, however, let me turn my attention briefly to two early Christian monastic codes and the way they contributed to an equally distinctive 'form-of-life' for the communities that adhered to them.

Early Christian monastic codes as form-of-life

In 4th-century Egypt, Pachomius' establishment of a rule-based monastic community was an innovation, a social experiment motivated by a divine call. The *Life of Pachomius* tells the story of how he began his days as a monk pursuing an intensive, semi-solitary ascetic life under the tutelage of an anchorite-mentor named Palamon. One day, while searching for pieces of wood in the desert, Pachomius came upon an abandoned village at a place called Tabennesi and received a vision from God exhorting him to 'Stay here and build a monastery, for many will come to you to become monks.' And so, Pachomius persuaded his mentor Palamon to accompany him to this new place, where he established his rule and began to attract a growing community, the first of several regional monastic foundations under his leadership.

The fact that Pachomius established his first monastery by reclaiming and refurbishing an abandoned village is not an incidental detail. Indeed, the social organization of the earliest Christian monasteries may be compared to that of towns or villages, insofar as they incorporated residential structures akin to households, streets and water distribution systems, agriculture and food production, industrial installations, infirmaries, and places of worship. In Chapter 5 I will discuss archaeological evidence related to these aspects of monastic life, but we already get a glimpse of at least some of them in the Pachomian *Rules*, or *Precepts*.

To accommodate his monks, Pachomius established a highly organized house system: he assigned to each a housemaster and labelled them according to the letters of the Greek alphabet (alpha, beta, gamma, delta, etc.). The houses were the setting for 'lesser weekly services' (complementing the 'greater weekly services' in the church), as well as for instruction given by the housemasters three times a week. Each house had cells, which were assigned to the monks as sleeping quarters: in these spaces, no speaking or eating was allowed. Doors had to remain unlocked, and no one could enter without knocking nor could anyone leave during sleep hours without special permission or 'in a case of necessity', such as an emergency visit to the latrine.

Outside the houses and cells, monastic life was regulated according to specific patterns of worship, work, and mealtimes. At the assembly of the community in the church, monks would recite passages from Scripture and participate in prayer litanies, but they were also instructed to keep their hands busy by weaving ropes for mats or palm leaves for baskets, and at the end of the service the superior of the monastery and each housemaster would inspect and keep record of their labour and production. After the assembly, there were designated times for work, and the housemaster would lead his charges out to their assigned tasks, while they recited Scripture or remained silent. Some Pachomian monks went on errands outside the walls of the monastery, while others had specialized roles within the monastic community as ministers to the sick (infirmarians), porters, gardeners, cooks, harvesters, bakers, boatmen, and stewards.

Many of these jobs had to do with the needs of food production and distribution, and the rules closely monitor the quantities served at mealtimes and the places where food could be eaten. Monks were afforded equal portions. The refectory was the primary venue for meals, but with special permission small supplements could be taken back to the individual monastic houses. In the infirmary, special diets were administered to the sick. In certain circumstances, monks could partake of food outside the monastery when travelling or paying a visit to a sick relative, or in the garden and orchards when harvesting fruits and vegetables. Food was never to be eaten in a monk's cell, however.

The stipulations regarding food and special care for the sick in the Pachomian monasteries are reminiscent of certain statutes in the *Bhikkhu Pātimokkha*, where the rules set conditions for what could be eaten by sick monks, and whether and when monks could eat in public rest houses and in groups, accept food as offerings from families, partake of successive meals or extra portions, and store food up for meals at non-standard times.

Also reminiscent of the Buddhist monastic code is the way the Pachomian *Rules* seek to shape a particular set of bodily dispositions. This entails a particular attention to dress and posture: accordingly, each monk is to 'sit with all modesty and meekness, tucking under his buttocks the lower edge of the goat skin which hangs over his shoulder down the side, and carefully girding up the garment...in such a way that it covers his knees'. It also involves refraining from speaking or laughing while in the church, house, refectory, or places in between, and avoiding bodily contact with other monks—not sitting together with another monk on a mat or carpet, not holding hands, not drawing a thorn out of another monk's foot, not shaving another monk's head, not even riding a bareback donkey together. At all times, monks were to leave a forearm's space between themselves and other monks, and when it comes to women—whether lay visitors or the nuns of a sister monastery—the rules mandate an even stricter, and closely monitored, separation. This mandated segregation of the sexes would become a characteristic feature of most later coenobitic communities, the most extreme example of which is Mount Athos, an entire peninsula in northern Greece reserved for male monastics where from its early medieval foundation women (and all female animals) have been forbidden entry.

Indeed, as mentioned earlier, the Pachomian *Rules* would set a pattern for virtually all rule-based Christian monastic foundations to follow. Pachomian-inspired communities spread from Egypt and Ethiopia to Constantinople, and from Greece and Italy to Gaul. This influence continues to be felt in modern popular culture: Umberto Eco, in his now-famous debut novel, *The Name of the Rose* (1980), set his story in a medieval Benedictine monastery in northern Italy where the abbot 'follow[ed] the ancient counsels of Saint Pachomius'.

But to understand how the Pachomian *Rules* could be adopted and adapted by other communities, we need look no further than across the Nile. Shenoute's federation of the three monasteries (two male and one female) was founded by a Pachomian monk named Pcol in the 4th century, and a close examination of Shenoute's writings shows how the rules governing his community incorporated (and expanded upon) key tenets of Pachomius' monastic code. Indeed, Bentley Layton has carefully documented how the monastery's leadership similarly micromanaged matters of food distribution and consumption, as well as interrelated concerns about the nutritional care for sick bodies. The parallels to the Pachomian strictures are striking: from forbidding extra portions and unauthorized foods, to establishing special dietary measures for monks who are ill.

But even more striking is the shared concern for guarding against not only heterosocial but also homosocial bodily contact. Shenoute explicitly borrows from the Pachomian *Rules* four times in his writings, and three of these pertain to this concern: prohibitions against shaving the head or extracting a thorn from the foot of another monk, and regulations about maintaining a cubit's distance from other monastic bodies. In Shenoute's *Canons*, however, this monastic vigilance about the dangers of physical proximity is considerably heightened and palpably sexualized. He graphically recites curses against any monk who spreads himself on top of or under another monk in his sleeping quarters, who embraces or kisses another monk with desire, who touches or grasps his own or another monk's penis, or who anoints or washes a sick monk while experiencing desire (and vice versa).

While such warnings were often framed in terms of male–male contact, there is ample evidence to show that Shenoute administered parallel admonitions to the members of the women's monastery in his federation as well. Thus, he curses 'whoever, whether it be male or female, shall sleep in pairs on a *tam-tam* mat or . . . close together, so as to touch and bump against one another with desirous passion'. Likewise, on three successive occasions, he condemns 'whoever among us, whether male or female', found running after neighbours 'with longings of the flesh and carnal friendships', or concealing such friendships from others. Perhaps the best example of how Shenoute's rules expanded in scope to cover any eventuality is his curse against 'males or females who stare and direct their eyes with desire at the nakedness of their neighbors in their sleeping quarters or . . . anywhere else'. The rule then goes on to itemize the possible scenarios where such voyeuristic desire might take place within the monastery: while the spied-upon monk is 'on a wall, up a tree, releasing a watercourse, trampling mud, washing themselves in water, sitting down and unconsciously uncovering themselves, pulling down a piece of wood from a high place, working with one another, or fulling their *hoeite*-garments in the washtub beside the canal or by the cistern, or . . . reaching into the ovens, or any other task that any people in our (men's) domain or your (women's) domain undertake and unconsciously uncover themselves'.

This hyperintensive focus on maintaining bodily boundaries and on monitoring the micro-textures of monastic life had a set of social effects. It created a community in which binary gender distinctions were rigidly maintained through the careful surveillance and systematic subjugation of sexual desire. In Shenoute's federation, same-sex desire was especially marked as a danger that would disrupt the economy of monastic bodies at work and at prayer, that would undermine the safeguards maintained by an unambiguously gendered, male/female segregation. Thus, the 'form-of-life' cultivated in Pachomius' and Shenoute's rule-based communities involved not only the external regulation of tasks and schedules, but also the internal, bodily dispositions that shaped male and female monastic identity.

The limits of monastic obedience

Discussing the Pachomian monastic rules in her book, *Porneia: On Desire and the Body in Antiquity*, Aline Rousselle describes them in terms not too dissimilar from Agamben's notion of a 'form-of-life' when she writes, 'Where we see in the rules a repressive command, in reality it was something which all the monks wished to see imposed,... to help them live the life they had chosen.' Yes, but did *all* monks embrace the rules? In one crucial sense they did, insofar as they vowed to live their lives in accordance with the rules upon entrance into the monastery. This common vow or commitment was the community's *raison d'être*. But at the same time, the very existence of the rules themselves mutely attests to the fact that sometimes monastic men and women diverged from the standards set by 'the life they had chosen' and enacted forms of active or passive resistance. Here is where we encounter the limits of monastic obedience. And yet, far from being outliers or exceptions to the rule, such acts of disobedience should be understood in fact as part and parcel of the monastic 'form-of-life' comprised and cultivated by the rules.

How exactly did such limits cultivate a 'form-of-life' that effectively incorporated communal expressions of both obedience and disobedience? To answer this question, we may helpfully draw on the work of Tudor Sala, who has studied early Christian monastic rules in terms of systems of surveillance. These systems aspired to a 'totalizing' perspective—an environment of complete visibility similar to the Panopticon prison complex developed by Jeremy Bentham in the 18th century. In the Panopticon, the design of the building allowed a single guard to observe all the inmates, while the inmates themselves could never tell whether they were actually being watched at any particular moment. The cumulative effect was that inmates would end up monitoring their own behaviour *as if* they were under surveillance at all times. According to Sala, the physical spaces and rules systems of early Christian monasteries created an analogous environment where the monks' obedience was motivated by their perception of 24/7 scrutiny—by their monastic superior, by their housemaster, and by their fellow monks.

One of the most interesting aspects of Sala's research, however, is his recognition of the way that monasteries negotiated the limits of their totalizing vision in and through the rules themselves. As evidence for such limits, the rules themselves sometimes show anxiety about places within the monastery conspicuously hidden from view, whether it be in the darkness of a monk's cell, or under the cover of blankets, or even in undetected furtive glances in broad daylight. These are blind spots in the surveillance network. But the rules also offer an effective counter: the all-seeing eye of God, which penetrates all spaces, which never rests and never sleeps, and which serves as implicit motivation for monastics to resist temptation and check themselves before committing acts of disobedience and attracting a divine curse.

One might apply these same insights regarding social visibility and the function of rules to the study of the *Pātimokkha* in Buddhist monasticism. At the beginning of the rules for both male and female monastics, there is an introductory section on the recitation of the *Pātimokkha* in which the participating monastics are exhorted to reveal any offences they may be guilty of. If there existed no offence to confess, they were to remain silent. But this, of course, leaves open the possibility that someone may remain silent in order to conceal an offence. So, the instructions continue by providing three opportunities to confess, 'but if any bhikkhu [or bhikkhunī], when it is being proclaimed up to the third time, on remembering it, should not reveal an offence which exists, it is a conscious lie for him [or her]', which is deemed to be 'an obstructing matter', something that prevents the state of purity requisite for continuing in the rite. In the rules for women, however, there is a clause added later (not found in the men's rules) to prevent one nun from concealing the fault of another: 'Whatever bhikkhunī, knowing that a bhikkhunī has committed a matter entailing defeat, should neither herself reprove her, nor speak to a group, but [if her concealment is revealed later], she too becomes defeated.' In these cases, and elsewhere, the operating assumptions of the *Pātimokkha* hinge not simply on external demonstrations, but also on internal assumptions: to have concealed a fault (whether one's own or another's) is to be guilty already of an obstructing matter or a matter entailing defeat.

In this way, both early Buddhist and early Christian monks and nuns would have engaged with rule-based monastic existence according to a daily calculus in which both the honours accorded obedience and the consequences resulting from disobedience were part of the same differential equation. To put it another way, the rules themselves, taken in the aggregate, would have fostered sets of bodily practices, dispositions, and resistances that constituted for members of these communities totalizing or all-encompassing 'forms-of-life'.

Chapter 4
Saints and spirituality

For monastic communities living together under a shared
system of governance, we have seen how rules function as both
the framework and texture for monastic practice, delimiting
boundaries for behaviour and establishing rhythms for bodies
living in close proximity to one another. As such, monastic rules
constitute a 'form-of-life' for monks and nuns seeking to pursue
a life of withdrawal and renunciation. But when it comes to the
cultivation of specific virtues—whether defined in terms of
holiness, purity, or perfection—Christian, Jain, and Buddhist
monastics have also had other cultural and ethical models to
draw on, including charismatic ascetic virtuosi who inspire acts
of imitation and veneration. In this chapter, we turn to the
privileged role that saints and their stories play in the shaping
of monastic spirituality.

Defining 'sainthood'

The word 'saint' comes from the Latin word *sanctus*, meaning
'sacred' or 'holy'. In the history of Western Christianity, this
language came to be applied not only to places (*loca sancta*) and
objects (*res sancta*), but also to persons who were understood to
be endowed with a special form of holiness. The corresponding
Greek adjective, *hagios*, is the root for the technical term,
hagiography, which refers to the literary genre of 'writings about

holy persons' (i.e. saints' *Lives*). In antiquity, the word *hagios* connoted not simply moral purity but the quality of being specially 'set apart' by or for God and thus the object of ethical imitation and reverence. Accordingly, Athanasius began his *Life of Anthony* by exhorting his readers both to 'emulate' and to 'marvel at' the saint's asceticism.

Similarly, the 5th-century Latin writer Sulpicius Severus framed his *Life of Saint Martin of Tours* as an attempt to 'write the life of a most holy man, which shall serve in future as an example to others', presenting him as 'a man worthy of imitation'. By the end of the work, Severus had shifted his purpose to that of extolling and expressing awe at Martin's saintly attributes: 'How insignificant is all such praise when compared with the virtues which he possessed...to such an extent did all the excellences surpass in Martin the possibility of being embodied in language.' As Robert Cohn has put it, this 'tension between imitability and inimitability'—between 'likeness' and 'otherness'—speaks to something fundamental about the social function of saints.

There is no single equivalent to the word 'saint' in the non-theistic Jain and Buddhist traditions of ancient India. The closest linguistic analogues, however, may be found in the Sanskrit terms, *jina*, *arhat*, and *bodhisattva*.

In Sanskrit, *jina* (from which the word 'Jain' itself derives) means 'conqueror'. It refers to someone who has vanquished all inner passions and the cyclical bondage to violence, and who thus has attained a form of omniscience. Paradigmatically, Mahāvāra is described as someone who 'knew and saw all conditions of the world, of gods, men, and demons, whence they come, whither they go,...all conditions of all living beings in the world, what they thought, spoke or did at any moment'. In the Digambara Jain tradition, attaining the rarefied state of *jina*-hood is associated not only with comprehensive mental insight, but also with the renunciation of physical and worldly ties, including the need for clothing, food, and sleep. As Natubhai Shah has noted, devotion to the *jinas* among Jains involves intertwined acts of imitation and veneration. Monks 'emulate' the lives of such figures in 'prayer, meditation, and conduct', and many also 'worship' the *jinas*, venerating their images through the recitation of names, the composition and recitation of hymns, and the making of offerings.

In both Jain and Buddhist contexts, an *arhat* is one who has been deemed worthy or deserving of transcending suffering and attaining a state of complete self-realization (i.e. *nirvana*). In the *Kalpa Sutra* (2nd or 1st century BCE), one of the most important canonical texts for Svetambara Jain monks, Mahāvāra is described not only as a *jina* but also as an *arhat*. In early Buddhist literature, some of Gautama Buddha's companions were likewise accorded this status. During the late ancient period (*c.*386 CE), however, the question of who deserved to be called an *arhat*—including what limits there were to an *arhat*'s virtuosity—became hotly contested and led to schism in Buddhist communities. Among Theravādin Buddhist monks, the title of *arhat* still continues to be used as a high honorific for those who are capable of attaining *nirvana*. By contrast, Mahāyāna Buddhist communities understand *arhats* still to be limited by certain mundane forms of human weakness, and instead place a greater emphasis on the role and status of *bodhisattvas*.

The term *bodhisattva* is composed of two Sanskrit roots—*bodhi*, meaning 'awakened, enlightened'; and *sattva*, meaning 'being'—and thus marks those who are destined to attain full enlightenment. (In the Theravāda tradition, the word is often used to refer to the Buddha himself prior to achieving transcendence.) A *bodhisattva* practises the six 'perfections' (*pāramita*), which include generosity, morality, patience, perseverance, meditation, and insight. In some Mahāyāna traditions, four more perfections are added to the list: skilful means, resolution (or vow), power, and knowledge. Taken together, these ten 'perfections' correspond to ten stages of spiritual development, which start with joy and purity and

culminate in the Dharma-cloud, a final stage that is likened
to ascending a throne and receiving a crown, and to receiving the
light of fully awakened wisdom and showering it down like
rain upon the world. To attain this state, monastic practitioners
must revere and worship the Buddha and follow in the footsteps
of *bodhisattva*s who have already paved the path towards
enlightenment.

Lives of monastic saints and ethics of imitation

In the ancient Greek world, the value of imitation (*mimēsis*) as
an ethical model was a frequently discussed and debated topic.
In his Socratic dialogue, *The Republic*, Plato writes about the
limitations of *mimēsis* as a method for attaining divine truth.
In Book 10, he discusses Socrates' teaching about three kinds of
beds. The first is the ideal notion of 'bed' in the mind of God.
The second is the physical or material form of the bed made by a
carpenter. The third is an artist's painted rendering of a bed.
For Plato, neither the carpenter's nor the painter's version of the
bed can ever capture the true essence of 'bed' as it exists as a
divine concept or idea. As such, for Plato, acts of imitation are
inadequate and derivative, falling short of perfection as the
philosopher's highest goal. This is one of the reasons why
he banished artists and artisans from the population of his
ideal republic.

By contrast, Aristotle held a somewhat more optimistic and
flexible view of *mimēsis* as a pathway towards perfection. In his
Poetics, he distinguishes rote copying from more advanced forms
of 'simulated representation'. In this context, he discusses the
effect that dramatic tragedy has on its audience: it causes its
viewers to identify and empathize—to participate vicariously—with
the characters and events being represented. As 'the imitation
of an action', it arouses pity and fear with the goal of 'effecting the
proper purgation (*katharsis*) of these emotions'. For Aristotle,
mimēsis as a form of representation had to be similar to and yet

different from the audience's life experience, simultaneously familiar and unfamiliar, if it was to have this kind of cathartic effect.

Early Christian Greek communities inherited this recognition of both the possibilities and limitations of imitation with regard not only to literary or artistic representation, but also to religious practice. As objects of imitation, saints were, on the one hand, profoundly relatable and 'emulatable'. And yet, on the other hand, by definition they also transcended the everyday experience of even the most pious believers. There was a similar ambivalence in Jain and Buddhist circles, where saints were viewed, by turns, as imitable and inimitable—they were eminently worthy of imitation, but at the same time they typically exceeded the moral capacity of those doing the imitating and thus became objects worthy of veneration. Stories about saints traffic in this 'mimetic' space, where human and superhuman capabilities collide. In this way, acts of imitation and veneration simultaneously highlight relational structures of sameness and difference between saints and their devotees.

A large proportion of saints' *Lives* have been written by and for monks, and in composing and transmitting such stories monastic authors have typically promoted an ethic of imitation among their readers. As applied to the monastic calling, this ethic is crucially rooted in both past and present models.

First, this ethic traces its authorization back to the life and teachings of the religious founders and early heroes of the faith. From the earliest days of Christian monasticism, hagiographers—writers of saints' *Lives*—have cited Jesus as the ultimate prototype for monastic practice, from his forty-day temptation in the desert to his bodily sufferings on the cross. As Edith Wyschogrod has written, 'A background belief of virtually all Christian hagiography is that saints live their lives in the light of Christ's life. *Imitatio Christi* is...the command that guides saintly conduct.' This can be seen perhaps most vividly in *The Little Flowers of St Francis*, written sometime in the 1320s, over a hundred years after the saint's death in 1226 CE. The work begins by underscoring how Francis 'was conformed to Christ in all the acts of his life. For just as the Blessed Christ, when he began his preaching, chose twelve apostles to despise all things of this world and to follow him in poverty and in the other virtues, so St Francis, when he began to found the order, had twelve chosen companions who were followers of the most complete poverty.' Just as Francis was conformed to Christ, so too his followers mirrored back the sanctity of the apostles.

In this example, we see how such literature established genealogies of sainthood, mimetic chains that crossed generations, beginning with Christ and the apostles and culminating in saintly figures like Francis of Assisi and the Franciscan brothers who followed in his footsteps. An important link in this chain for the formation of Christian monastic identity was the chorus of early church martyrs, who suffered as Christ suffered and thus served in turn as a model for the suffering of monks. Through their metaphorical death to the world and their perseverance in bodily trials until their own death, the monastic faithful were understood to have inherited the martyrs' 'crown of righteousness' (2 Timothy 4:8). Thus, in one of the *Sayings of the Desert Fathers*, the voice of God tells an unnamed Egyptian monk after nine excruciating years of resisting temptation: 'These nine years during which you have been tempted were crowns for you.' Accordingly, Athanasius of Alexandria, in his *Life of Anthony* (ch. 47.1), describes how, after the early Christian persecutions had ended, the monk Anthony 'departed and withdrew once again to the cell, and was there daily being martyred by his conscience, and doing battle in the contests of the faith' through his 'more strenuous asceticism'.

In Jain and Buddhist monastic discourse, the founding figures Mahāvāra and Gautama Buddha play roles as authorizing paradigms for followers pursuing the monastic path. Thus, in the Jain *Kalpa Sutra*, the lives of different *jina*s are presented as the same life recapitulated over and over again, and in the Buddhist *Mahapadana Sutta*, the Buddha himself narrates the life histories of past Buddhas, who are said to remember what their predecessors did and to follow their example.

In medieval Jainism, however, such mimetic genealogical connections became rather complicated. Stories often presented accomplished monks as devotees of Mahāvāra, and yet at the same time as public figures drawn into the orbit of the royal court in ways that ran counter to earlier ideals of monastic withdrawal. One such example is the biography of the 14th-century monastic luminary Jinaprabhasūri, which describes how Jinaprabhasūri's 'many excellent qualities' mirrored Mahāvāra's own 'innumerable wonderful qualities'. And yet, Jinaprabhasūri's life was characterized by close proximity and access to the Muslim sultan's court. As the recipient of royal patronage, he lived in a specially built monastic residence right next to the sultan's palace and installed an image of Mahāvāra on the premises. In so doing, he is said to have 'emulated the accomplishments of the great monks who had preceded him', and his deeds are celebrated as 'exemplary' for those who followed in his wake. His biographer inserts him into this mimetic chain despite the fact that his lifestyle looked very different from Mahāvāra's rigorously ascetic withdrawal from the world.

Thus, we see how an ethic of imitation, with its valorization of sameness, could nevertheless find outlet in diverse expressions of monastic practice and piety. As John Kieschnick has noted, a very different ethos is cultivated in medieval Chinese hagiography, where stories abound of Buddhist monks who sought to emulate the Buddha in enactments of self-sacrifice. Just as the Buddha was willing 'to sacrifice himself for others' by throwing himself into the sea to feed the fish or by lying down before a tigress and her cubs (as told in Ārya Śūra's *Jātakamālā*), so too various Chinese monks were said to have surrendered themselves to the bites of insects (as a form of compassion for those creatures), to have offered their own flesh to hungry wild animals or starving villagers, or to have given up their lives to rescue a child from kidnapping or a monastery from looting. One full chapter of the early *Liang Biographies* is dedicated to monastic heroes who 'sacrificed their bodies' (*wangshen*). Among the various tales collected there is one about a monk named Tancheng who mutely imitates the Buddha by lying down in front of a tiger to save a village. He is eaten but the grateful villagers are left in peace. In China, such stories were often compiled after a monk's death by his disciples, who would then commission a skilled local writer 'to work this material into an ornate encomium'.

This brings me to my second point with regard to the ethic of imitation, as it has pertained to the production of saints' *Lives*. Namely, such an ethic is profoundly shaped not only by authorizing models from the past, but also by contemporaneous social structures, most notably the core relationship between mentors and their disciples. In receiving instructions from their elders, monastic apprentices are expected to obey without question or hesitation. As such, obedience becomes a cardinal virtue, a visible sign of the apprentice's desire to conform his or her actions to the mentor's example. Indeed, the transmission of stories about eminent monks may be seen as a natural extension of their disciples' reverent obedience to the legacy of their teachers. As Elizabeth Castelli notes, such mimetic relationships between teachers and students are typically 'hierarchical and asymmetrical', with the former privileged as a normative model and the latter necessarily in a subordinate position. But sometimes those dynamics can be inverted in unexpected ways.

Two brief examples from the *Sayings of the Desert Fathers* will suffice to illustrate the complexities of early Christian monastic discipleship. The first is a pithy statement by a monk named Moses that underscores the replicability of obedience as a mimetic practice: 'Obedience begets obedience; if someone obeys God,

God listens to him' (14.9). Here, the sense of Moses' teaching is twofold. On the one hand, the obedience exhibited by the mentor monk will be replicated in the obedience of the disciple. On the other, the obedience of the disciple will in turn foster a posture of responsiveness (understood here as a form of reciprocal obedience) on the part of the mentor, whether that be a wiser, older monk or an attentive God. A similar sort of code switching can be seen in a second example: a story from the same collection about a domestic slave who 'became a monk [and] lived for forty-five years content with salt, bread, and water'. His rigorous ascetic commitment prompted his original owner to adopt the same lifestyle: 'his master withdrew [from the world]...and he became the disciple of his own slave, [serving him] in great obedience' (14.31). In these two examples, monastic sainthood is framed in terms of mimetic obedience, but this obedience can sometimes take a reciprocal form that upends and restructures the core mentor–disciple relationship.

In the *Lives* of Jain and Buddhist saints, such mentor–disciple relationships are complicated by family lineages and the fact that the path to enlightenment in those tales sometimes spans several lifetimes. Thus, one Jain story about 'The Monk Sukośala' tells of a king named Kīrtidhara who becomes a monk and 'wanders from place to place, performing extreme asceticism', his body 'emaciated from fasting'. His bald head shone with 'a special lustre that had been imparted to it by the ritual of plucking out his hair that he had performed when he renounced the world'.

During his wanderings, Kīrtidhara comes to the house where his wife Sahadevī and his son Sukośala lived. Sahadevī chases him away so that her son would not be attracted to the monastic life, and she bans all ascetics from the city. When his son Sukośala learns of his visit, however, he seeks out his father. Finding him, he asks him to make him his disciple: 'Consecrate me as a monk under your tutelage.' The son plucks out his hairs, a renunciatory act that notably mimics his father's own original ritual gesture, and then, having 'received the vows of the monk from his preceptor', he sets out with this father.

The rest of the plot narrates how the father and son—now mentor and disciple—withdraw to the forest for the traditional rainy season retreat before resuming their wandering life. As such, the story presents their ascetic path as a paradigm and pattern for later Jain monastics to imitate. The tale finally concludes with a complication and a happy resolution. Sahadevī—Kīrtidhara's wife and Sukośala's mother—dies and becomes a tigress in her next life. When she encounters the two monks on the road, they stand still in 'a posture of meditation', but she pounces on her former son and devours him from head to toe. As a result of his steadfastness, Sukośala become 'Omniscient' and is 'released from his body'. His example leads his father to gain omniscience as well, and the tigress is finally 'awakened to the Truth by Kīrtidhara's gentle words'. After renouncing everything, she 'died a pious death' and 'went to heaven'. Here, once again, the mimetic chain is shown to flow in both directions. Having followed his father on the path to renunciation, the younger disciple later leads his father-turned-monk on the path to omniscience, and his mother-turned-tigress to a state of awakening.

In an influential article entitled 'Mimesis and Violence', René Girard perceptively notes that 'mimetic rivalry tends toward reciprocity. The model is likely to be affected by the desire of his imitator. He becomes the imitator of his own imitator.' But Girard also observes that the urge to imitate can lead to violence between antagonists, a situation of conflict only resolved through the mediation of a scapegoat. In the case of Sukośala's story, the boy imitates his father's asceticism and succeeds to such an extent that he ends up being the one to guide his father to a shared condition of omniscience. At the same time, his mother becomes his mimetic rival for his father's companionship, and violence ensues. The scapegoat in the story is Sukośala's own flesh, which his mother-turned-tigress tears apart and devours until he is 'released from his body'. This bodily sacrifice is what is required to resolve the conflict: the mother-tigress is awakened and renounces the world after the pattern of her son and husband, and a promise of happiness is extended to the reader as well, if he or she 'learns about the greatness of Sukośala'. Girard's insights into the complicated relationship between imitation and violence have been applied to early Christian monastic texts as well, where (as Brian Robinette puts it) the triangulations of 'mimetic desire...can [also] tend either toward creative mutuality or violent rivalry, with many different shades in between'.

Ascetic saints, spiritual combat, and the making of monks

Girard's observations about the relationship between mimesis and violence may be extended further in light of how monastic narratives often portray the ascetic life as a form of spiritual combat. Saints held up as exemplars for monastic imitation are often portrayed as engaged in martial contests with human and non-human foes. We have already encountered the image of an early Christian desert father being equipped for battle with the armour ('breastplate') of God, and the Jain monk Sukośala achieving victory by allowing his body to be torn to shreds by a vicious tigress. What role does the representation of spiritual combat play in the *Lives* of holy figures, and how does this relate to the portrayal of saints as mimetic models for the monastic life?

In his scholarship on the early Christian 'holy man', Peter Brown provides a helpful set of tools for answering these questions. For Brown, the representation of saintly figures in the late Roman world was about the adjudication of social and spiritual power. The *Lives* of saints represent them in various roles, each of which sheds light on the way that they functioned as channels of divine potency and *charisma*. As miracle workers, holy persons make their power manifest in imitation of Christ. As arbitrators and mediators between God and humankind, holy persons hold the power to 'lift the vengeance of God' by removing the effects of a curse or exorcizing a demon. As strangers to society, they stand 'outside the ties of family, and of economic interest', and thus personify a kind of objective authority, similar to that of the ancient Greek oracles. As healers and confessors, they bring the divine near to human supplicants by offering cures and blessings. As patrons and friends of God, they sponsor an economy of gift exchange, serving as intercessors and ambassadors at the divine court on behalf of their faithful clientele and receiving their devotion in turn. As preachers of repentance, they hold sway over human hearts, 'stirring [them] to contrition'. As privileged liaisons between the human and natural worlds, they calibrate the order and balance of the cosmos. Finally, as ascetic athletes, holy persons train their bodies into powerful vessels for the rigours of renunciatory existence, which sometimes takes the form of visceral, violent combat with demons and other opposing forces.

To get a more textured sense of the role that competition and combat play in the literary representation of saints as models for the monastic life, and how ascetic practice is portrayed as a venue for the exercise of spiritual power, let us turn to the biographies of two famous solitaries, one from late ancient Egypt and the other from medieval Tibet. The first is Anthony, the desert hermit and so-called 'father of Christian monasticism'. The second is Milarepa, the revered Buddhist yogin and wandering teacher.

At the beginning of the *Life of Anthony*, its author Athanasius addresses his readers, praising them for having 'entered on a fine contest with the monks in Egypt, intending…to measure up to or even surpass them in [the] discipline of virtue'. These readers had asked Athanasius about 'the career of the blessed Anthony', that they might 'lead [themselves] in imitation of him' and 'emulate his purpose'. Thus, from the start, Athanasius frames his work as being designed to foster imitation of Anthony as a model of one who contended in a monastic 'contest' (Greek, *hamilla*). The word he employs here typically designates athletic competitions, including races and feats of strength. Other similar vocabulary is used throughout the *Life* to describe Anthony's ascetic struggles, including the Greek noun *athlon* ('contest') and the Greek verb *agōnizesthai* ('to fight, struggle, compete for a prize').

The portrayal of Anthony's monastic life as a contest or competition is exemplified by his clashes with demonic forces. During his early ascetic practice, Anthony endures repeated attacks and temptations by the devil, who beset him with 'memories of his possessions, the guardianship of his sister, the bonds of kinship, love of money and of glory, the manifold pleasure of food, the relaxations of life, and, finally, the rigor of virtue'. The *Life* depicts Anthony as engaged in a battle over the power of memory, with recollections of life's pleasures ('a great dust cloud of considerations') at war with his memory of Scripture as a guide to virtue.

This visceral spiritual combat is described as simultaneously an internal and external struggle. Satan 'hurled foul thoughts' at Anthony, or beset him with 'titillation', and Anthony would fend off these temptations through prayer and fasting. The devil first assumed the form of a seductive woman and later appeared to Anthony as a 'black boy' (an ancient ethnic stereotype adapted here and elsewhere in early Christian monastic literature as a cipher for sexuality and erotic power). In each case, Anthony successfully resisted the temptations posed and thus prevailed in his 'first contest (*athlon*) against the devil'.

Doubling the intensity of his ascetic practice, Anthony relocated to the tombs well outside his village and arranged for friends to provide him with bread for sustenance. There he was attacked by demons with even greater ferocity: he was whipped 'with such force that he lay on the earth, speechless from the tortures'. Later, when he locked himself in his cell, the demons transformed into a menagerie of beasts and made terrifying noises, raging against him and wounding him in his body.

After these trials of sexual desire and physical assault came temptations of money and wealth. When Anthony moved to a 'mountain' and 'a deserted fortress', the devil laid a silver dish and pieces of gold along his path. But Anthony was not distracted, nor did he grow tired of the 'contest' (*agōnizesthai*). His renown as a monastic combatant attracted the attention of many aspiring monks, who 'possessed the desire and will to emulate his asceticism', and as a result, 'there were monasteries in the mountains and the desert was made a city by monks,... and like a father he guided them all'.

The *Life of Anthony* concludes by emphasizing how this 'multitude of ascetics' were of 'one mind' as they 'aspired to become imitators of his way of life'. The end of his life was marked by the performance of various miracles: he made demons (in the form of hyenas) flee with a word; he healed a paralysed young woman; he was instantaneously transported from one bank of the Nile to the other; he demonstrated clairvoyance; he prayed and relieved a woman from stomach pain; he experienced divine visions; he exorcized demons and cured people of mental illness. All of these acts elicited responses of wonder and amazement from his disciples and other observers. Indeed, the final chapters of Anthony's *Life* negotiate a delicate balance between describing how monks imitated his example and how he became a subject of veneration in both life and death.

The *Life* ends by emphasizing that Anthony became 'famous everywhere...in Spain and Gaul, and in Rome and Africa'. In fact, the *Life* itself became the primary vehicle for the spread of Anthony's monastic example across the Mediterranean. Athanasius' work became the closest thing to a *New York Times* bestselling novel in the early Christian world. Within the span of only a decade or two, Gregory Nazianzen, the bishop of Constantinople, referred to Anthony's example, calling Athanasius' biography 'a rule of monastic life in the form of a narrative' (*Or.* 21.5).

Translated into Latin, the *Life* would eventually come into the hands of Augustine during his time in Milan. In Book 8 of his *Confessions*, Augustine tells the story of how a Christian named Ponticianus ('who held a high position in the Emperor's household') paid him a visit in his home and told him the story of 'Anthony, the Egyptian monk'. Augustine had never heard about Anthony before, or about the existence of such monastic communities in the desert. Ponticianus told Augustine how, during a garden stroll outside the city walls of Trêves (modern Trier), two of his friends had come upon a house where some monks lived, and there they found 'a book containing the life of Anthony'. Picking it up and reading it, one of them abandoned his career and became a monk. After reading further, the two jointly decided to relinquish 'all they possessed'. Later, the two friends told Ponticianus of how they had 'dedicated their virginity' to God.

Hearing this story from Ponticianus caused Augustine's conscience to gnaw at him and prompted him to walk out into the garden where his famous 'conversion' took place. In fact, what Augustine narrates in his autobiography is as much a monastic calling as it is a conversion—a calling modelled after that of Anthony. Augustine hears 'the sing-song voice of a child in a nearby house' repeating the refrain, 'Take it and read, take it and read', and interprets this as a 'divine command' to open his Bible and read the first passage he finds.

This interpretation is specifically inspired by Anthony's story. Augustine writes: 'I remembered how [Anthony] had happened to go into a church while the Gospel was being read and had taken it as a counsel addressed to himself when he heard the words *Go home and sell all that belongs to you. Give it to the poor, and so the treasure you have shall be in heaven; then come back and follow me.* By this divine pronouncement, he had at once been converted to you.' Immediately thereafter, Augustine opened a scriptural book containing Paul's letters and read a passage from Romans 14:1, which exhorted him to eschew 'reveling, drunkenness, lust, wantonness, quarrels, and rivalries', to 'spend no more thought on nature and nature's appetites', and to 'arm' himself (as if for spiritual combat) 'with the Lord Jesus Christ'. This scriptural/ oracular message—a textual variation on Anthony's aural revelation—led Augustine to retire from teaching, to withdraw to a life of contemplative retreat, and eventually to found his own monastery in North Africa.

Augustine's experience is just one example of how Anthony came to serve as the preeminent mimetic model for the Christian monastic calling. In medieval and early modern Europe, Anthony's battles with demonic temptation would later serve as the inspiration for the monastic Order of St Anthony, which established a network of hospitals to care for people afflicted with a disfiguring ailment called St Anthony's fire. In this order, Anthony's reputation as a healing saint became the subject of iconography, including a painted panel on the famous Isenheim Altar (c.1515; Alsace, France), where Anthony is depicted sitting in the desert surrounded by medicinal herbs and fighting demons afflicted with the characteristic pustules of the disease (see Figure 4). Applied to settings ranging from art to medicine, saints like Anthony proved to be eminently adaptable in the pieties and practices of later monastic communities.

As a subject for hagiography, the Tibetan Buddhist ascetic Milarepa (1028/1040–1111/1123 CE) offers an interesting counterpoint for comparison. Despite the fact that his rigorous renunciatory practices, commitment to a life of solitude, and attraction of disciples bear certain resemblances to that of Anthony, in the Tibetan cultural context Milarepa is not considered a monk, but rather a yogin. This distinction is crucial and yet complicated when it comes to the representation of Buddhist holy figures.

In Tibet (and throughout the Buddhist world), monastics are persons who take vows of ordination indicating their obedience to a canonized monastic rule (the *Vinaya Piṭaka*) and who thus

4. Painting of St Anthony's battle with demons, by Mathis von Aschaffenburg (Isenheim Altar, *Temptation of Saint Anthony*, 1512–16).

yoke themselves to a residential community (*sangha*) populated by other ordained monastics. In the history of Christianity, ascetic hermits and their counterparts living under a communal rule have both traditionally qualified as 'monastics', but this is not the case in the history of Buddhism, where 'the monk or nun is not an independent ascetic' but rather someone who dedicated his or her life to being part of a religious community. A Buddhist yogin (or a female yoginī) is one who is dedicated to the practice of meditation (yoga). Such a figure can live a solitary, celibate life, but this is not necessarily the case. Some yogins establish small communities, taking on the role of lamas (teachers of the path, or *dharma*). Others associate themselves with previously existing temples or monasteries. Some maintain active sexual lives in conjunction with meditational practices, as is true with certain forms of tantra (a form of ritualized meditation involving the visualization of deities). As such, yogins could occupy a range of social niches within local Buddhist communities.

As we shall see in the case of Milarepa, he straddles a number of the aforementioned categories: in his biographies, he is identified as a yogin, a lama, and a practitioner of tantra. Milarepa's meditational practice as a yogin stands in opposition to the monastic communities of his day, which were critiqued as too caught up in contemporary politics. And yet, Milarepa's biographers also sought to present his life as an example for monastic readers to imitate, as a model for implementing alternative ways of being a monk. Milarepa is also honoured as a lama in his role as a teacher and mentor to a community of disciples. And yet, like Anthony, his aspiration was to separate himself and practise his austerities in solitude. Finally, as a practitioner of tantra, Milarepa demonstrated certain 'supernatural' or miraculous powers over the natural environment and other people, but in contrast to some of his contemporaries (including his own guru Marpa) he specifically eschewed marriage and sex in his commitment to an ascetic path. This crossing or blurring of categories is one of the factors that have contributed to Milarepa's status as the Tibetan holy man par excellence. Another is his heroic reputation for overcoming karma and attainment of liberation over the course of a lifespan, a trajectory that his biographers specifically model after that of the Buddha.

I refer to biographers in the plural because several medieval versions of Milarepa's biography survive. Two of the earliest narratives about his life were written by his 12th-century disciples, Ngendzong Repa and Gampopa. Later versions would incorporate poems attributed to Milarepa himself. By the 13th and 14th centuries, literary compendia such as *The Twelve Great Disciples* and *The Black Treasury* combined 'structured and well-crafted biographical narratives ... with extensive song collections', as well as 'elaborate descriptions of the yogin's death'. These were the primary sources that paved the way for what became the standardized version of Milarepa's *Life*, written in the 15th century by Tsangnyön Heruka (1452–1507), the iconoclastic tantric lama who called himself the 'Madman of Western Tibet'. In what follows, I briefly trace the contours of this biography, paying special attention to how the *Life of Milarepa* came to serve as a mimetic (and somewhat transgressive) model for Tibetan Buddhist piety for a wide readership that included monastic audiences.

Tsangnyön Heruka's *Life of Milarepa* is divided into two parts. Part One consists of the first three chapters and concerns Milarepa's problematic conduct prior to his decision to seek the path to transcendence. Part Two consists of chapters four to twelve and narrates his sufferings under his teacher Marpa, his reception of the *dharma* instruction, and his life of meditation and self-abnegation leading to full enlightenment.

Chapters one to three describe Milarepa's genealogy, birth, and upbringing in a wealthy family. His happiness in childhood was interrupted by the death of his father when he was seven years old, and by his family's subsequent oppressive treatment at the hands of his paternal uncle and aunt, who took their possessions and forced them into abject servitude. Desperately mired in poverty and encouraged by his mother, Milarepa turned to black magic to enact revenge upon his relatives. Having sought out and studied with two lamas specializing in such arts, Milarepa casts a spell that kills thirty-five guests at the wedding feast for his nephew, sparing his uncle and aunt only so that they would know the consequences of his retribution. Later he sends a hailstorm to destroy all the crops in his uncle's village. These malicious acts of revenge serve as the backdrop for Milarepa's remorseful decision to repent, renounce the world, and seek out a lama who will teach him the true *dharma* path to enlightenment.

The first three chapters of Part Two (chapters 4–6) tell the story of his search for a teacher of *dharma*. After two different teachers prove insufficient, Milarepa ends up at a 'remote hermitage' at the feet of Marpa Lotsawa, who is identified as 'a direct disciple of the great Indian adept Nāropa'.

Marpa becomes Milarepa's mentor, but subjects him to a draconian series of commands meant to prove his mettle and his preparedness to receive the oral teachings of *dharma*. Marpa conscripts him to hard labour, commanding him to build four towers and then to tear each one down before he is able to finish. Marpa also resorts to verbal humiliation and physical violence, rebuking Milarepa, beating and kicking him, and throwing him to the ground. As a result, Milarepa's back bled and 'festered with sores'. In the midst of these depredations, Milarepa finds inspiration by reading the biography of Taktungu, a famous *bodhisattva* 'who, while penniless, was able to renounce life and limb for the dharma'. Eventually, Marpa relents, accepts him formally as his disciple, and reveals his larger purpose: 'I have only tormented [Milarepa] in order to purify his negative deeds'. To mark his new status as a yogin, Milarepa has his head shaved, changes his robes, takes the vows of a layperson, and receives 'the bodhisattva precepts'.

The remainder of Part Two (chapters 7–12) narrates Milarepa's life of meditation, solitude, and arduous mortification of his body, a path that leads to full enlightenment at the time of his death. Inhabiting a series of remote caves, he pursues a strict ascetic regime, persistently refusing to take a wife and instead committing himself to practise the *dharma* in emulation of his teacher. In Heruka's biography, Milarepa's austerities serve as an explicit critique of the 'worldly pride' of monks (those who wore 'golden' or 'saffron' robes and who get distracted by 'wealth and fame'). At first, Milarepa's diet consists of gruel (only one load of barley flour a year). Later, he survives only on nettles. As a result, his body 'became like a skeleton…covered with soft green hair'. His clothes hang in tatters and eventually fall off. He makes these rags into a 'modesty sleeve' for his penis; otherwise, he remains naked. When his devoted sister comes to visit, she finds him wasted away, with eyes 'sunken into their sockets', with his 'bones stuck out'. One of Milarepa's songs included in the *Life* (ch. 10) goes so far as to compare him to a 'rotting corpse unseen by vultures'. And yet, despite these signs of physical deterioration, Milarepa demonstrates tremendous feats of bodily control, including 'transforming [his] body into any desired form and levitating in space…transforming [his] body into blazing fire, gushing water, and the like', and even transporting his body from one place to another in flight.

The final two chapters of Heruka's *Life of Milarepa* catalogue his human and non-human disciples and his places of retreat (which became destinations for pilgrimage visitation and meditation among his followers), and then tell the story of his death by poisoning. His biographer underscores the fact that the poison had its effect only with his consent. Up until his final breath, Milarepa remains in control: he miraculously transports his body to various places to appear before his disciples, he confers his staff and robes upon his disciple Rechungpa, and he orders his body to be cremated. When he dies, 'dissolving his body into the sphere of reality', he proves worthy to have achieved enlightenment.

Throughout the standard version of his *Life*, Milarepa is presented as one who mirrors the Buddha himself and likewise serves as an exemplary model for his followers, among them monastic communities who appropriated his legacy. The structure and ending of Milarepa's biography underscore the connection with the Buddha's example. Just as the Buddha performed twelve great deeds, beginning with his birth and ending with his passing into *parinirvāṇa*, Milarepa too is said to perform twelve 'supreme deeds', which correspond to the twelve chapters of his *Life*. Chapter one in the *Life of Milarepa* begins with the phrase *E ma ho* ('Thus did I hear ...'), which is the same phrase attributed to the Buddha's cousin and close disciple Ānanda, words that signified 'his perfect recitation from memory of the Buddha's teachings at the first monastic council'. Indeed, Milarepa is described by one of his own disciples as a buddha or bodhisattva 'from the start'. Finally, Milarepa's death replays key elements of the Buddha's passing: his death by food poisoning; the failure of the funeral pyre to light until the appearance of a beloved disciple; and a dispute among his followers over the cult of relics.

This mimetic framework is reinforced in Milarepa's relationships with his mentor Marpa and with his cadre of disciples. These relationships constitute a 'dharma lineage of enlightened activity'. The *Life* emphasizes the 'pristine connection' between master and student: they are 'equal in kindness' and their 'minds ... are intermingled'. His followers are exhorted to 'follow [his] example and practice' by meditating in the places where he meditated and by transmitting his sacred biography. In this context, one of his songs extols 'those who act and practice with my life in mind, those who write or teach or listen to it, read it or pay it respect, and those who emulate my life'. Indeed, the biographer Tsangnyön Heruka himself would later be celebrated as a privileged incarnation of Milarepa, with one 13th-century historian (Chökyi Wangchuk) noting an incarnation lineage—'a series of manifestations with identical qualities'—that culminated with Heruka.

Despite the fact that Milarepa's biography was framed as a critique of complacent monastic practice, ordained Tibetan monks in fact played prominent roles as devotees and literary caretakers of his memory. Six of Milarepa's closest disciples were fully ordained monks, and the *Life* itself concludes with a colophon identifying the work as 'a feast for monks who renounce the world' as well as 'a feast for renunciants who've relinquished attachments'. One of his closest followers, Gampopa Sönam Rinchen, was responsible for 'promoting Milarepa's tradition of yogic practice within a monastic framework', and scores of monks played an instrumental role in composing, editing, copying, and preserving the various versions of his *Life*. Milarepa's literary lineage extended to female monastics as well. One notable case is Orgyan Chokyi (1675–1729 CE), a nun from Dolpo, Nepal, who was the first documented woman to write an autobiography in Tibetan. As Kurtis Schaeffer has observed, this 'Himalayan hermitess' partially modelled her own life story—especially its recurrent themes of tears and suffering—after Heruka's biography of Milarepa.

As in the case of the Christian St Anthony, we also have examples of how Milarepa's legacy was reappropriated in the visual culture of Buddhist monks. One of the earlier proto-versions of his *Life* contains painted illustrations that subtly reshape the yogin into a monastic saint. On one folio, both his mentor Marpa and his disciple Gampopa are depicted in the robes and hats of monastic scholars. Elsewhere, other disciples of Milarepa are depicted in the distinctive garb of fully ordained monks with their right hands raised to their ears in a gesture of singing, a posture clearly meant to copy Milarepa's standard depiction. Such representations established a 'direct equivalence' where the monastic image of the devotee stood in for (but also redefined) the image of the saint. Thus, we see how even a non-monastic saint could serve as a mimetic model for monastic piety, but at the same time how monastic devotees could reshape the image and legacy of that same saint to their own purposes.

Chapter 5
Spaces real and imagined

Home is where the heart is. In contemporary American culture, the phrase has become ubiquitous. Framed on the walls of family rooms, cross-stitched on throw pillows, written in cursive script on coffee cups: the phrase attempts to capture the sense of attachment, belonging, and close connection that nuclear families feel towards their living spaces. Oddly enough, this same phrase could easily serve as a motto for many monastics who have left their natal homes and families to find alternative places of residence, whether in deserts or forests, whether alone or in a community.

In a blog dated 11 October 2011, Benedictine Sister Ann Marie Wainright reflected on a new postulant's questions concerning the size and layout of nuns' cells—questions that prompted memories of the day she moved into her own room in the convent years before. Composing her blog entry in that same cell with sunlight streaming through her window, she wrote, 'If *home is where the heart is*, then I was at home—not just in my room, but in the heart of God.'

This same connection was made by early Christian monks. In the 4th century, one of the most prominent monastic centres in Egypt was a settlement called Scetis (Wādī al-Naṭrūn), located west of the Nile Delta. Scetis is the setting for many stories in the *Sayings of the Desert Fathers*, including one anecdote about the monk Moses the Black. One day, Moses tells one of his brothers: 'Go, sit in your cell, and your cell will teach you everything.' In this teaching, the cell is conspicuously presented as an extension of the monastic self. That is, for Moses and his compatriots, you are where you live. This insight is also reflected in the geographical nomenclature for Scetis itself. In the indigenous Coptic language, the region is known as the 'Weigher of Hearts' (*Shiēt*, from the roots, *shi*, 'weigh, measure', and *hēt*, 'heart'). For the monks of Scetis, their desert cell was the place where their hearts were weighed in the balance by God.

With this close relationship between residential spaces and monastic identities in mind, I now turn to the locations where monks and nuns live in community: monasteries. First, I will focus on monastic archaeology. What can material evidence tell us about monks' and nuns' places and modes of habitation, from architecture to agriculture, from practices of visitation to visual culture? Second, I will also examine monastic stories and art to mine the meanings that such landscapes and homescapes had for their resident populations. What did the cell, the monastery, the desert, and the forest, signify for the monastic imaginary? How have local spaces imprinted themselves on monastic pieties, and vice versa?

The archaeology of monasteries

I begin with the material evidence for monastic places of habitation. Historically, monks and nuns have shown a remarkable ability to adapt their physical environments to suit their own needs. Such settlement patterns are attested in literary sources as well as the archaeological record.

In Buddhist and Christian *Lives* of eminent monks and nuns, ascetics frequently occupy remote caves to pursue a life of renunciation and meditation. In the Chinese biography of Bo

Sengguang, for example, the 4th-century Jin monk withdraws to a cave on Mount Shicheng—later known as Hermit Peak—in the province of Shan. There he is haunted by 'the spirit of the mountain'. In the *Life of St Benedict*, a 'narrow cave … overhung by a high cliff' in Subiaco, north-east of Rome, serves as the Italian monk's initial retreat. There he is tempted by the devil.

Other stories describe how monks reclaimed and occupied previously existing architectural structures. In the *Lives* of Anthony and Pachomius, a deserted fortress and an abandoned village are respectively reclaimed for monastic practice. But of course, monastic communities also constructed structures from scratch, planning and building their architecture to specification. Thus, early stories about the Buddha describe financial negotiations for the donation of land used for the construction of new stupas and monastic retreats; and for early Buddhist communities, the *Bhikkhu Pātimokkha* establishes standards for 'having a large dwelling place made', including specifying acceptable locations, the proper amount of plaster, and the placement of doors and windows.

The archaeological evidence for monastic settlements attests to a correspondingly diverse range of architectural and residential practices. Here, it is helpful to think in terms of two different patterns for the physical construction of monastic spaces: first, adaptive reuse of the environment; and second, purpose-built architecture.

In their natural state, caves make for rather inhospitable settings for human habitation, and this is the reason stories about monastic heroes often highlight the threat of exposure and danger associated with such spaces as a constituent component of ascetic renunciation. But in practice, it seems likely that even the most hardened cave-dwelling hermits adapted their physical environments in basic ways to suit their needs. (If they hadn't, there would be no tangible evidence to confirm they had ever been there!)

Architecturally speaking, such adaptive reuse could take a form as simple as the building of a low enclosure wall for privacy, or the levelling of a ledge to be used as a bed. But it could also take more elaborate forms, as in the case of rock-cut monastic complexes from ancient India, Nepal, and China, to early medieval Egypt and Italy.

One of our earliest pieces of evidence for the modification of caves into monastic dwellings comes from 3rd- or 2nd-century BCE Nepal, where a number of rock-hewn huts from the period have survived at a site named Gum Bahal, which translates as 'The Monastery of Caves'. These huts are 'small boxlike structures' consisting of two chambers: an entrance vestibule and a sleeping area. Since even the task of excavating the rock mass to create small square chambers would have necessitated a significant investment of time and money, archaeologists think that such huts would have been occupied by high-ranking monastic teachers. A group of seven caves in Bihar, India, may date from even earlier, probably to the middle of the 3rd century BCE. The most prominent of them is the Grotto of Lomas Rishi: carved and initially occupied by a sect of Jain monks (Ajivikas), it has a hut-like façade designed to look like timber.

Other surviving rock-cut *vihāras* in India and China show a more expansive and refined architectural plan. At the monastic sites of Pitalkhorā and Bhājā in Maharashtra, the rock has been carved to mimic ornate wooden architectural designs. Later *vihāras* from the same region show how caves were opened up into central arcaded courtyards, with ten to twenty cells arrayed around the outer borders, and decorated with sculptures and painted panels. One especially complex example (Ellora Cave 12) has three storeys, approximately thirty small chambers and/or shrines, and a pillared hall measuring around thirty-five square metres in area. At Ajaṇṭā in western India, thirty-six caves carved into a 250-foot-high rock face became home to monks around the turn of the Common Era: by the late 5th century (460–80 CE) an elaborate artistic programme had been executed on the cave walls, including colourful paintings of the lives of the Buddha and sculpted reliefs of nymphs, sea monsters, and genies. Around the same time in China, rock-cut monasteries became way stations for missionaries bringing Buddhist teachings to that region. One such station were the Mogao caves at Dunhuang, which feature ornate sculptures and paintings, including scenes of the Buddha's incarnations.

One finds analogous adaptations of natural space in Christian cave monasteries as well. At an Egyptian site called Naqlun in the Fayoum Oasis, for example, excavators have discovered a total of eighty-nine rock-cut hermitages dating from the 5th to the 12th century and carved out of the porous tufa that forms the hills and ravines bordering the oasis. Designed for one or two occupants, the hermitages at Naqlun consist of multiple rooms, often plastered, in various sizes and shapes: these could include vestibules, inner and outer courtyards, windows, sleeping quarters, cooking areas, storage spaces, and prayer rooms. The lack of ovens for baking or facilities for storing wine and water suggests that the hermits living there had to depend on deliveries of foodstuffs from the walled monastic community situated nearby.

In Italy, the 'Sacred Cave' (*Sacro Speco*) at Subiaco legendarily associated with St Benedict's early monastic life provides an interesting comparison. There are no solid archaeological data regarding its period of origin, but surviving evidence confirms that the cave was (re)inhabited by hermit monks in the late 11th century. By the turn of the 13th century a regular monastic community had been established there, and the cave church had become the subject of significant architectural and iconographic modification. From the medieval period to the present, the monks in residence have admitted pilgrims to the site, and visitors have been able to tour a multi-level monastic church carved out of the rock and decorated with an extensive wall-painting programme, including scenes from the life, death, and resurrection of Christ, and from the life and miracles of St Benedict. The lower level of the church features the 'Sacred Cave' itself, where Benedict was reputed to have begun his career as a monk. The walls of this holy grotto have been left as bare stone, which spatially conveys to visitors a sense of unmediated access to the monastery's founding figure.

When it comes to their places of residence, monastics have not only adapted caves and other features of the natural landscape. They have also designed monasteries as purpose-built architecture. When made with less permanent materials like wood or mud brick, such structures have not often survived for archaeological study. But those that do survive give us a picture of diversified monastic forms and functions.

Purpose-built Buddhist monasteries may incorporate various architectural elements. As in the case of rock-cut cave sites, architecturally designed *vihāra*s have typically been configured as 'a series of cells enclosing three sides of a square courtyard'. But monastic complexes can, and often do, include other elements, including worship halls (*chaitya*s), stupas, refectories, and connecting pathways.

In India, early examples show how these elements were often arranged in a north–south orientation, with flanking buildings to the east and west. The ancient monastic sites of Thotlakonda and Bavikonda in north coastal Andhra Pradesh, India, for example, are laid out along a similar axis. To the north is an area featuring a main stupa and worship hall. To the south lies a courtyard or cloister with a colonnaded hall at its centre, which is surrounded on three sides (east, west, and south) by residential cells. Further to the east is a refectory complex.

A similar 'bilateral symmetry' has also been observed at the Horyu-ji monastery (7th century CE) in Nara, Japan, where a 'golden hall' and a pagoda are placed on either side of a central axis leading towards a lecture hall to the north. In Japan such structures are characteristically raised on a stone platform (or an ascending series of platforms), and sometimes pagodas are located away from the central axis, outside exterior walls, or hidden among trees. At Horyu-ji, the monastic campus also integrates a range of other buildings, including a dormitory, dining hall, library, lecture hall, and bell tower.

The emphasis on architectural symmetry in the design of Buddhist monastic sites was conditioned, in part, by aesthetic factors, as well as the contours of local topography. In one notably idiosyncratic case, at the 11th-century Byōdō-in monastery outside Kyoto in Japan, one of the halls is designed 'in the form of a phoenix with outstretched wings' hovering over a reflecting pond within a beautifully manicured park. In his study of Buddhist monastic architecture in Sri Lanka, Senake Bandaranayake likewise describes an 'organic' layout in which built structures were integrated with and served as an extension of their natural environment. Later in this chapter, we will see how architectural landscapes became the subject of spatial imagination in monastic literature and art.

Purpose-built Christian monastic architecture also exhibits a diversity of forms, which may be divided into two main categories: the smaller-scale 'cell'; and the larger-scale walled enclosure or 'monastery' proper. The former is analogous to domestic houses that serve as places of residence for individuals or small family units. As such, 'cells' typically incorporate rooms or spaces for sleeping, cooking, eating, receiving visitors, and private prayer. The latter is analogous to villages that accommodate communities of monks or nuns living and working together. As such, 'monasteries' often incorporate not only dormitories, kitchens, refectories, guesthouses, and churches, but also walls and gates, administrative and storage buildings, industrial and manufacturing facilities, wells with plumbing and irrigation systems, agricultural plots and orchards, streets and alleyways, and many other features common to small towns or large estates.

A paradigmatic example of the first category—the 'cell'—is the early Christian monastic settlement of Kellia on the western outskirts of the Egyptian Delta. In Greek, the word Kellia in fact means 'cells', and the settlement took shape as a large cluster of small dwellings. In its heyday between the 4th and 8th centuries CE, the Kellia settlement covered more than forty-nine square miles and hosted upwards of 1,500 monastic cells. Most of the surviving remains date from the 6th or 7th centuries.

The dwellings at Kellia were primarily constructed from mud brick and ranged considerably in size. Small cells accommodating one to three people could measure between 180 and 600 square metres. These structures were equipped with sleeping quarters for an elder monk and perhaps one or two of his disciples, a storeroom, and areas designated for work and prayer. Sometimes they would also feature a reception area and an open courtyard, sometimes with a garden, well, and/or latrine. Medium-to-large cells accommodating anywhere from five to ten hermits could range from 700 to 2,700 square metres. These dwellings had open courtyards, larger halls for assembly, and more ornate decorations, including faux-sculptured columns and painted wall murals.

An analogous settlement pattern may be observed in Wādī al-Naṭrūn (ancient Scetis). Since 2006, the Yale Monastic Archaeology Project (YMAP) has conducted surveys and excavations at the Monastery of John the Little, where the remains of around eighty mud-brick residences dot the landscape outside a central walled enclosure with a main church. The site shows how two types of monastic organization—independent cells and a communal monastery—could coexist in practice. The work of the Yale team has concentrated in particular on one monastic cell measuring twenty-five by twenty-five metres (Residence B) and dating to the 9th and 10th centuries CE. The structure contains twenty-five rooms, including primary and secondary kitchen spaces, organized around a central courtyard. Among its rooms is one with prayer niches, an extensive wall-painting programme featuring equestrian martyrs and monastic saints, and several painted inscriptions.

For an example of the second category—the communal, walled 'monastery'—we may turn to YMAP's work at the White Monastery in Upper Egypt. In late antiquity, the White Monastery was part of the federation of three monasteries headed in the first half of the 5th century CE by Shenoute of Atripe, whose rules we studied in Chapter 3. The White and Red Monasteries were communities of male monks, while a convent in the village of Atripe to the south was home to female nuns. Since 2008, Yale has conducted surveys and excavations at the White Monastery, and in 2016 we initiated work on the remains of the women's community at Atripe.

Located at the foot of the cliff at the western edge of the Nile Valley, the White Monastery resembled a village in physical layout and social organization. The monastery was bordered by an enclosure wall and accessed through a gate monitored by a doorkeeper. Inside the gate, the monumental 5th-century Church of St Shenoute, which still stands today, served as the central place of assembly and worship, and probably housed the monastic library (see Figure 5). Another chapel within the complex may have been designed as Shenoute's burial place and shrine.

To the south, west, and north-west of the main church, archaeological remains provide evidence for facilities that would have allowed the monastery to be virtually self-sufficient. These facilities included industrial installations for the processing of olive oil and dyes, kitchens with millstones for grinding grain and eleven or twelve bread-baking ovens, refectories for meal gatherings, dormitories for sleeping, a treasury building that combined administration and storage functions, and a huge well with an elaborate water distribution network. During Shenoute's time, the monastery also maintained agricultural plots, orchards, and animal pens. Such a complex and extensive system of buildings and landholdings would have required constant

5. The monumental, 5th-century Church of St Shenoute at the White Monastery (Sohag, Egypt), viewed from the east.

administrative upkeep and a cadre of specialists (monastic or otherwise): industrial workers, bakers, cooks, servers, administrators, plumbers, farmers, tenders of livestock, and of course architects, civil engineers, and builders.

The women's monastery at Atripe, located about five kilometres to the south of the White Monastery, shows how such communities could accommodate hybridized forms of architecture, with both adaptive reuse and purpose-built structures in evidence. Thus, the church at Atripe was built into the previously existing Ptolemaic temple in the town, but other monastic buildings—including a six-pillared hall and a large refectory with multiple circular eating spaces—were built outside the temple walls. Painted inscriptions (*dipinti*) analysed in 2016 and 2017 confirm that these spaces were used by female monastics, and that matters of food distribution remained a central concern. In one case, a young novice named Evangelia wrote a note on the wall of the refectory

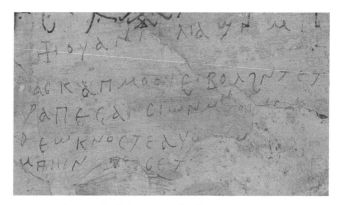

6. Late ancient Coptic *dipinto* (painted wall writing) by a young nun or female monastic apprentice named Evangelia on the wall of the refectory in the Shenoutean women's monastery at Atripe (near Sohag, Egypt).

documenting her role in sending water and food out to members of the community (see Figure 6):

1. Little Evangelia
2. sent out the water from the
3. table of Zion, along with the food, to
4. Theōgnoste and […]
5. of the house of [sheph]erds (?) who […]

Medieval Christian monasteries in Europe developed their own distinctive architectural patterns to meet a similar range of everyday needs. Plans were typically organized around a central 'cloister' (from the Latin *claustrum*, 'enclosure'). In early medieval Europe, as illustrated by the Plan of St Gall (820 CE), the cloister took the shape of a square colonnaded arcade or covered portico, bordered on one side by the monastic church and enclosed on the other sides by two-storey buildings containing a variety of facilities: dormitories, warming and cooling rooms, refectories, vestiaries, cellars, and larders. Smaller buildings at the corners could house lavatories, bathhouses, kitchens, bakeries, and breweries.

Other variations included chapter houses (i.e. meeting rooms).
The fundamental purpose of the cloister was to segregate the
monks or nuns from the outside world.

Of course, different monastic orders adapted this monastic plan
to their own purposes in different ways, and these adaptations
had implications for the physical layout, land use, and labour.
At the Abbey of Cluny, founded in 910, an increasing emphasis
on liturgical service led to architectural renovations that amplified
and accentuated the *maior ecclesia* (the 'Great Church'). Beginning
in the 12th century, the Cistercian reform movement shifted the
emphasis, simplifying the liturgy and assigning manual labour to
all members of the community, which included both monks and
lay brothers. As a result, the monastery plan had to incorporate
separate quarters outside the cloister for the lay brothers.

Cistercian monasteries such as Cîteaux and Clairvaux were often
established in secluded, undeveloped settings, where the members
of the community had to reclaim the land by clearing forests and
planting fields. Once a monastery was established, it was the lay
brothers—working in the buildings, fields, and water systems
outside the cloister as masons, millers, fullers, weavers, bakers,
tanners, smiths, farmers, shepherds, plumbers, and civil
engineers—'who enabled the early Cistercian communities to be
self-supporting'. In this way, Cistercian monastic foundations
could become economic and social centres.

Such was the case at Hailes Abbey in Gloucestershire, England,
founded by the Earl of Cornwall in the 13th century. Its extensive
landholdings included orchards and fish ponds, and its huge
(104-metre-long) church hosted a vibrant pilgrimage industry
centred around a contact relic, a phial of Christ's blood kept in a
shrine behind the holy altar.

Thus far, I have discussed the material realities of monastic
archaeology and architecture, the physical spaces inhabited by

monks and nuns. Such spaces imposed constraints upon movement and daily practice, but they could also be adapted through architectural renovations designed to address new needs in the community. An important part of monastic practice is the challenge of negotiating such spatial constraints, of defining (and redefining) the relationship between oneself and one's physical environment. And yet, the spatial dimensions to this process of monastic identity formation cannot simply be reduced to the empirical distance between the walls of buildings. Monastics have also had an active hand in reimagining and mythologizing their physical environments, and this is the subject that will occupy our attention for the rest of this chapter.

Imagining monastic spaces and landscapes

If cells are extensions of the monastic self, they have also been understood as places that mediate contact and union with the divine. As Anthony was credited with saying: 'Just as fish die if they stay too long out of water, so the monks who loiter outside their cells or pass their time with men of the world lose the intensity of inner peace.' For their inhabitants, cells and monastic enclosures prove to be more than the sum of their material parts: they carry symbolic and spiritual value, reinforced through ritual practice. The architecture of monasteries is informed not only by site plan but also by embodied theologies.

In the case of Christian monasteries, such spiritual or theological value can be seen in the way that cruciform spaces shape the contours of worship and everyday life. One interesting example is the Monastery of St Simeon in north-west Syria. As mentioned in Chapter 2, Simeon (390–459 CE) was a holy hermit whose ascetic regime involved living on top of a 21-metre-tall pillar. Hundreds of pilgrims came from near and far to see the spectacle, to catch a glimpse, and to seek the blessings of the holy man. To accommodate the flow of visitors, a monastery with a hostel grew up around his column. The monastic church was laid out in the form of a cross with Simeon's pillar at the midpoint. For pilgrims after his death, the architecture communicated that Simeon's monastery fulfilled the promise of Christ's crucifixion, simultaneously marking the centre of the world and pointing the way to heaven.

One also observes a symbolic negotiation of the horizontal and vertical in the medieval monastic churches built by the Knights Templar, a military order of warrior monks established in the 12th century who played an instrumental role in Crusader campaigns to the Holy Land. The order's circular or polygonal churches were modelled after the temple and Christ's tomb in Jerusalem. Prominent examples include the Holy Sepulchre in Cambridge (*c*.1130), the Temple Church in London (1185), the Templar Chapel in Laon, France (*c*.1180), and the Convent of Christ in Tomar, Portugal (late 12th century). Worshippers in these spaces understood themselves to be vicariously present as witnesses to the events of Christ's life, death, and resurrection in the Holy Land, even as the high arches of the sanctuary space drew their focus upward to God.

Buddhist monasticism has trafficked in similar symbolic constructions of sacred spaces, where architectural structures mediate local and universal access to the holy. The establishment of monasteries at the sites associated with eight major events in the Buddha's life mapped out an itinerary of *loca sancta* for pilgrims in northern India, linking those monastic foundations to their founding figure. The cyclical nature of such connections was reinforced and 'summarized in eight set scenes (*baxiang*)' commonly represented in hagiographical literature and art. One such iconographical example is a pigmented stone sculpture from Bodhgaya—now housed at the Rubin Museum of Art in New York—depicting the Buddha under the *bodhi* tree at his moment of enlightenment, with the other seven scenes depicted in miniature around him. Sometimes sculptures carved into the fabric of the walls themselves also prompted viewers to imagine monasteries as divine palaces and paradises, as in the case of the rock-cut Cave 16 at Ajaṇṭā in India, modelled after the heavenly abode of the god Indra.

The layout of Buddhist monasteries also sometimes provides universalizing coordinates for practitioners within the space. Perhaps the most paradigmatic example is the monastic use of the maṇḍala as a model for architecture and ritual practice.

Maṇḍalas are diagrams—carved into stone, or carefully plotted out in sand—that under some circumstances provide tantric practitioners with a means to visualize and attain enlightenment. Originally altars that were set into the floor as seats for the deities and their images, maṇḍalas came to be 'envisioned as elaborate, bejeweled three-dimensional palaces atop Mount Meru, the imagined center of the Buddhist world system'. They are typically constructed in layers and concentric rings, with the centre and its four prongs representing the five victorious Buddhas, or *jina*s.

While the use of maṇḍalas is not restricted to monastic practice, Buddhist monks have long incorporated them into their architecture and ritual life. Two rock-cut cave monasteries (Caves 6 and 7) at Aurangabad in Maharashtra (north-western India) were designed in the form of esoteric maṇḍalas. Elsewhere in the same region, in Cave 12 at Ellora, an early eight-bodhisattva maṇḍala has been carved into the stone. Monks living and meditating at these sites thus would have understood the monastery itself to be 'a cave in the side of Mount Meru, reaching the very core of the world-system axis'. Lindsay Jones has described this as the 'architecturalization' of the maṇḍala: at such sites the very act of moving through the temple or monastic space is implicitly framed as a figurative and psychological journey through both the universe and one's own consciousness. In Tibetan monasteries, monks and nuns contemplate two-dimensional maṇḍala wall hangings and paintings and painstakingly create multicoloured maṇḍala diagrams out of sand (see Figure 7), while invoking deities and presenting offerings (food, flowers, incense, fire, water, etc.). These are acts that ritually mark the interior of the monastery as a rarefied space for attaining a purified state of wisdom and compassion leading to full enlightenment.

7. Tibetan nuns from the Keydong Thuk-Che-Che-Ling Nunnery (Kathmandu, Nepal) create a sand maṇḍala at Davis Museum, Wellesley College (23 February 2005).

In the artistic and literary imagination of monks and nuns, the landscape outside the monastery enclosure also comes to be viewed as sacralized territory, as an extension of the divine union realized within. The forest or desert surroundings are thus transformed—from a foreboding reminder of the world and its threats, to a verdant spiritual paradise.

Medieval Chinese Buddhist artists frequently depict monasteries in idyllic mountain settings, nestled among trees by clear-flowing streams. One example is a painting by the 17th-century artist, Shitao. Entitled *Light of Dawn on the Monastery*, the artist uses an ink-on-wash technique to depict a scene in which the monastic buildings are nestled among pine trees and dwarfed by soaring mountain peaks with craggy summits stretching up into the heavens (see Figure 8).

金光朝霞
清湘石濤已有夏日寫於
歙安之紫陽書院

8. Painting depicting a Chinese Buddhist monastery in an idyllic mountain landscape.

A written account of the Dajue Monastery in Luoyang, China, could just as easily describe the unidentified monastery represented in the painting: 'The grounds were auspicious, sacred, and truly scenic...[and the monastery] backs on the mountain.' Indeed, Chinese inscriptions and historical records often attend closely to the significance of topographical and natural features in and around the monastic foundation. Thus, a stone stele highlights how the intersection of rivers, marshes, and mountains mark the 'sacred confines' and 'blessed ground' at the Shaolin Monastery. Similarly, a *Record of Buddhist Monasteries in Luoyang* notes the presence of aromatic plants, evergreens, hollies, water lilies, and mallows at the Yaoguang Nunnery. In an entry on the Yongning si Monastery, the same source describes how the cypress, juniper, and pine caress the building, and celebrates the fact that 'the beauty of the cloisters' exceeds the heavenly 'Palace of Purity'. Elsewhere, it dwells on the sweet and fragrant fruits, including pomegranates and grapes, that flourish at monastic sites.

James Robson has used the term 'geopiety' to describe such accounts. They capture the Chinese notion of *fengsu* (Japanese, *fengshui*), which places value on the intersection of the natural environment (*feng*) and human actions (*su*) performed within that environment. In this context, for monks or nuns seeking an auspicious place for monastic contemplation, location mattered. Landscape and practice mirror one another: the macro-cosmic paradise without reflects the micro-cosmic paradise within.

The monastic landscape as paradise is a theme found in Christian literature as well. Perhaps the best example of this is the Coptic *Life of Onnophrius*. It tells the story of a monk named Paphnutius who journeys into the far reaches of the desert trying to find the fabled hermit, Onnophrius, who wanders the wilderness naked and lives in a small hut under a date palm, subsisting on a diet of plants. When he finds him, Onnophrius tells his visitor how the Lord provided him with 'twelve bunches of dates' each year and 'made the other plants that grow in the desert places sweet in my mouth, sweeter than honey in my mouth'. After receiving instructions, Paphnutius is sent back to his own community at Scetis to share his teachings with the brothers there. On his way home, he runs across a well of water surrounded by an oasis of trees, including 'date palms...laden with fruit' and 'citron and pomegranate and fig trees and apple trees and grapes and nectarine trees', as well as 'some myrtle trees...and other trees that gave off a sweet fragrance'. Walking among them, Paphnutius asks himself 'Is this God's paradise?' (*Life* 28–9). Thus, as Tim Vivian has argued, the *Life* effectively presents the desert as a 'paradise regained' by anchorites like Onnophrius, who have returned to the original innocence of Adam and whose heroic piety has made the barren wasteland fertile again like the Garden of Eden.

This vision of monastic sites as Edenic persisted through the medieval period and into modern times. The 12th-century Latin authors Honorius Augustodunensis and Hugh of Fouilloy envisioned monasteries as earthly paradises, likening 'the body of the Lord' celebrated in the Mass, and the evergreen planted in the cloister lawn, to the Tree of Life. Their contemporary, the Benedictine abbess and mystic, Hildegard of Bingen, wrote that monastic virgins—in both their buildings and their bodies—remained 'in the unsullied purity of paradise'. Hildegard famously composed liturgical hymns for her German convent that were meant to 'recall to mind that divine melody of praise which Adam, in company with the angels, enjoyed in God before his fall'.

In the Christian East, for centuries, the sayings of the early desert mothers and fathers have been transmitted under titles such as *The Paradise of the Fathers* and *The Garden of the Monks*. These collections continue to be used as training manuals in monasteries and convents today. Finally, in contemporary North America, Catholic publishers now print devotional volumes like David Keller's *Oasis of Wisdom* (2005), where the early monastic heroes of the faith are presented as an Edenic wellspring of renewal for a church parched by modern secularism. In such publications, the places and practices of early Christian monks and nuns are reclaimed for 21st-century pieties of prayer and devotion, and it is to such modern monastic forms of expression that I now turn.

Chapter 6
A global phenomenon in the contemporary world

After the Protestant Reformation in the 16th century, monasticism in the Christian West fell out of favour and scores of monasteries were dismantled and destroyed. In 1521, Martin Luther published his treatise, *On the Monastic Vows*, in which he castigated his own previous vocation as a monk, calling it immoral and contrary to Scripture. As a consequence, in Germany a number of Augustinian friars renounced their vows. In his *Institutes* (4.13.14), John Calvin was equally critical, blaming the proliferation of monastic orders for the factionalism and disunity of the church. In 1536 (the same year Calvin's *Institutes* were published), King Henry VIII dissolved abbeys and convents in England, Wales, and Ireland, stripping them of their land, income, and assets. Once the economic bedrock of medieval Europe, monasteries quickly became disenfranchised, increasingly becoming a cultural afterthought.

Interestingly, around the same time, Near Eastern monasticism was also experiencing a significant decline due to a very different set of factors, from economic recession to population decline. In Syria, the Monastery of Qenneshre on the eastern bank of the Euphrates shut down during the late medieval period: once host to a thriving academy of theology and science, by the 14th century it was abandoned. In Egypt, the 15th and 16th centuries marked a period of decline, as the Monastery of John the Little (and many others) went defunct and fell into ruin.

The 18th and 19th centuries saw the rise of the European Enlightenment, with its emphasis on scientific rationality and suppression of religious 'superstition'. Those centuries were also the heyday of the imperialist and colonialist enterprise, with its forceful exportation of these ideologies to dependent territories in the Middle East, Africa, and Asia. By and large, modern intellectual and political forces were unkind to monastic causes in the West. And yet, the 20th and 21st centuries have notably witnessed the flourishing of monastic practice in a number of places across the globe. Why? What might explain this somewhat unexpected renaissance? In this concluding chapter, I seek to answer these questions by asking what difference monasticism makes in modern times.

To understand the role of monastic communities in today's world, we must first understand the emergence, and subsequent breakdown, of a particularly modern notion of 'religion'. On the one hand, as a category for organizing the world, 'religion' has been defined in sharp contrast to 'secular' spheres of life. On the other hand, as a global phenomenon, the domain of 'religion' has also been mapped out as a field of separate, competing 'world religions'. And yet, over the past two or three decades, scholarly research has shown the cracks and inconsistencies in such characterizations. When it comes to the study of monasticism in modernity, neither the religious–secular binary nor the world religions model proves adequate to the task. First, as we shall see, in the 20th and 21st centuries, monastic communities have frequently been swept up in public debates and forms of activism closely connected with national identities and spheres of life not traditionally deemed 'religious'. Second, during that same period, new hybrid forms of monastic practice have emerged that cut across and redraw boundary lines on the 'world religions' map.

Religion, nation, and monastic identity

The relationship between national politics and monastic identities in the 20th and 21st centuries has been complicated and multifaceted. From the Middle East to Asia to North America, monks and nuns have structured their lives in ways that have sometimes challenged the values of modern nations. But at the same time, the politics of the nation state as an 'imagined community' has also become imprinted upon the way that some contemporary monastics envision their own role in the world.

The idea of 'imagined communities' was coined by Benedict Anderson to describe nations as communities defined not by face-to-face interaction (due to their typically large size and scope), but rather by the creation of affinities, or co-citizenships, through shared public discourse. A famous example of how this works is the Tomb of the Unknown Soldier in Washington, DC. The significance of the grave is defined by a noticeable absence or lack. The personal identity of the individual interred there remains a mystery: if the soldier's bones were to be identified definitively, the tomb would no longer serve its purpose. It is the tomb's unknowability that allows it to function as a potent symbol of the nation's values of service, sacrifice, and heroism. This kind of symbolic national capital proves to be eminently adaptable, and in the case of contemporary monasticism one observes the multiple and malleable ways that such religious communities situate themselves in relation to governmental power. To illustrate how this works in practice, let me turn to a few examples focusing on the relationship between monastics and the state.

My first example focuses on modern Tibet. Since the 17th century, Tibetan monks—and especially the Dalai Lama, the monastic head of the Gelugpa sect—have played an instrumental role in the governance of that country. The Dalai Lama is revered as the incarnation of the *bodhisattva* of compassion, and for most of the period from 1642 to the 1950s a lineage of successive Dalai Lamas ruled Tibet from the capital at Lhasa. According to this theocratic form of rule, monasteries provide a counterweight to the interests of the state, a balance embodied in the person of the Dalai Lama himself.

But in 1951 everything changed. That year, China asserted sovereignty over Tibet under a '17-point Agreement' negotiated with Tibetan representatives of the Dalai Lama. Throughout the rest of the decade, however, the Chinese government's programme of nationalization divested monasteries of lands and properties, resulting in unrest and resistance led by Tibetan monks (and supported internationally by the CIA). The year 1959 marked a large-scale uprising against Chinese rule. The Dalai Lama publicly repudiated the '17-point Agreement' and went into exile in India, where he and his monastic followers established a number of transplanted Tibetan communities. What ensued was a series of government reprisals in Tibet during which hundreds of indigenous monasteries were bombed and hundreds of thousands of Tibetans lost their lives. The Cultural Revolution under Mao (1965–1975) led to the suppression of Buddhism and further destruction of monasteries. In subsequent decades, while a number of these destroyed foundations have been rebuilt and re-established in the Tibet Autonomous Region, many communities remain in exile, and monks continue to play integral roles in the Tibetan political resistance.

The role of monastic communities as a collective voice for Tibetan religious nationalism was epitomized in events that took place in Lhasa in the late 1980s. Protesting Chinese imprisonment of their compatriots, monks in the capital city decided to boycott the Mönlam festival, a New Year ceremony established in the 15th century to reaffirm the nation's commitment to Buddhism and the governing role of the Dalai Lama. Overseen by officials from the Drepung Monastery, the festival dramatizes a shift in locus of authority through a subversion or reversal of social functions. During the three-week rite, monks replace secular government officials, temporarily taking up the reins of government. This subversion ritually marks the state's submission to the monastic hierarchy, while also renewing and reaffirming monastic endorsement of Tibetan state authority. In the late 1980s, when China tried to insert itself as the official sponsor of the festival, the monks of Lhasa refused to participate, 'thereby denying the Chinese state legitimacy in its claim to be a patron of Buddhism'. Such acts of resistance not only forced the Chinese government's hand to commit resources to the restoration of monasteries; they also shaped the contours of a distinctively Tibetan nationalism among subsequent generations of Buddhist monks, who have understood themselves as the vanguard in a decades-long struggle for independence.

My second set of examples relates to Thailand, Myanmar, and Sri Lanka, where Buddhist nationalist movements rooted in monastic activism have sometimes tipped over into violence against other religious populations. In southern Thailand, monasteries have doubled as military bases for vigilante armies intent on suppressing an Islamic insurgency that broke out in 2004. In Myanmar, militant monks have aligned themselves with the Democratic Karen Buddhist Army and the 969 Movement, two organizations founded or headed by monastic leaders that have pursued campaigns of persecution targeting Muslims in that country. In Sri Lanka, Buddhist monks have also embraced violence as a means to suppress the Tamil, Christian, and Muslim minority populations. At the forefront of this nationalist effort in Sri Lanka is the Bodu Bala Sena, the 'Buddhist Power Force', founded by two prominent monastic leaders who had previously been associated with the right-wing National Heritage Party (Jathika Hela Urumaya).

Over the last decade, the Buddhist Power Force in Sri Lanka has incited communities of monks to mob violence and the demolition of mosques. In this case, such actions have received support from the country's hard-line government, which itself has engaged in a policy of reclaiming Islamic holy sites in the name of Buddhism. In one case, the culture ministry repurposed a Sufi Muslim cave by installing a stupa and claiming that the site had previously been a Buddhist monastery. Such actions are not unlike those of the early Christian monks who participated in the ritualized demolition and desecration of pagan temples. After such acts of destruction, they built and consecrated new churches within the former temple precincts as a means to wrest such spaces away from the 'demons' and to reclaim them for the Christian faith.

In places like Sri Lanka, competing visions of nationalist identity have led to divisions within the monastic population, with some monks taking a militant stance and others rejecting this path in favour of a more pacifistic politics. One such critic of militant monastic nationalism is the Sri Lankan monk Watareka Vijitha Thero, who was forced to hide out for almost a year from the threat of reprisal by other monks loyal to the Buddhist Power Force. In the end, his hiding place was found out, and he was kidnapped and left stripped, gagged, bloodied, and bound by the side of a road in an act of intimidation. Later, to add insult to injury, he was thrown in jail for almost two weeks, a further warning to those who would join him in his dissent against the Buddhist Power Force. Such intra-monastic conflict bespeaks radically different visions for how monks should relate to political force and the religious other.

For my third example, I turn to a community of Catholic nuns in North America—the Sisters of Social Service—whose commitment to public advocacy is rooted in the values of a liberal democracy. A leading member of this community is a nun named Sister Simone Campbell. Trained as a lawyer, she served as an attorney for the Community Law Center in Oakland, California, before being named executive director of NETWORK, a social justice organization staffed primarily by nuns who lobby for legislation related to housing and health insurance on behalf of the poor.

In April 2012, Sister Campbell's organization was singled out in a Vatican report condemning the errors of so-called 'radical feminist' nuns in the United States: at issue was NETWORK's silence on abortion and the church's 'right-to-life' policy.

Far from mutely submitting to the Vatican's chastisement, Sister Campbell chose to double down on her organization's political advocacy for socially liberal causes. During the summer of 2012, she took her message on the road as part of a two-week 'Nuns on the Bus' national tour with the goal of motivating 'opposition to a House [of Representatives] budget that would sharply reduce spending on social services' and sponsoring support of President Barack Obama's health care plan's contraception coverage (see Figure 9).

Notably, the 'Nuns on the Bus' tour did not restrict itself to the organization of local rallies, but also drew on a range of social media platforms to spread its message. Sister Campbell made guest appearances on *The Colbert Report* and *The Daily Show with*

9. **Sister Simone Campbell and the 'Nuns on the Bus'.**

Jon Stewart, where she received the gift of a 1950s-style black jacket with the words 'Bad Habitz' emblazoned on the back. The nuns also produced an online documentary promoting their tour and a YouTube music video entitled '#NunTrouble: It's All About That Bus'.

The music video illustrates the way that Sister Campbell and her monastic colleagues appropriated American popular culture for a cause that explicitly endorsed the assumptions of Western democracy. The song, 'It's All About That Bus' itself is a riff on the top-ten hit single, 'All About That Bass' by Meghan Trainor, with the same tune adapted to new lyrics. The original was a catchy, upbeat, and occasionally mildly profane celebration of the artist's body, highlighting her generous hips (and small bust size) as an antidote to female body shaming. Reworked by Sister Campbell and the 'Nuns on the Bus', however, the song takes on the character of a paean to social justice and voters' rights. In the video, the nuns and their co-workers travel around in their bus promoting voter registration. One scene shows them having fun dancing in a conga line, and even coyly plays off the sexuality of the original song with a suggestively silly scene that shows a nun's derrière in the proximity of a banana lying on an office filing cabinet. Here, the representation of female monastic identity—defined by a life of celibacy—parodies the media-stoked sexual proclivities of wider Western society.

As a cultural expression of monastic community, the 'Nuns on the Bus' are certainly a far cry from the exiled Tibetan monks resisting Chinese governmental policy, or from the militant monastics in Thailand, Myanmar, and Sri Lanka. But the vast cultural chasm separating these case studies should not blind us to the fact that for each of these groups, the politics of the modern nation state has served as a context for bringing monastic identity and practice into the public sphere.

Furthermore, as illustrated by the 'Nuns on the Bus', the dividing lines between 'religion' and 'popular culture' do not simply become blurred: they are exposed as artificially constructed and ephemeral. For Sister Campbell and her female monastic colleagues, to be a 'religious' is not simply to live a life of prayer but also to produce films and music videos that advocate for political justice. The end result is a hybrid cultural product—monastic identities formed at the intersection of religion, politics, art, and global media.

From monastic dialogues to hybrid monasticisms: the making and unmaking of modern religion

In his book *Genealogies of Religion*, Talal Asad writes about the creation of hybridities in history, noting the particular modern effects of mobility, translation, and cultural acts of borrowing and exchange. Monasticism has not been immune to these processes, and in fact these hybridizing factors have resulted in the production of multiple new ways of being 'monastic' in the late 20th and early 21st centuries. In the rest of this chapter, I explore this diversity further and, in the process, revisit my earlier questions about definitions.

On 4 November 1968, a meeting of two great monastic minds took place in the Himalayas. Thomas Merton, the famous Trappist monk and author of the bestselling autobiography, *The Seven Storey Mountain* (1948), was making a pilgrimage tour of monastic communities in Asia and had travelled to Dharamsala in northern India for an appointment with Tenzin Gyatso, the 14th Dalai Lama. Merton prepared for the visit by reading the poetry of the Tibetan saint Milarepa and the Dalai Lama's writings on Buddhism, but he came in with culturally laden suspicions. As Merton recounted in his travel journal, he had heard that the Dalai Lama had 'very few advisers who kn[e]w anything about the world as it is', and that his counterpart's retinue was filled with 'progressive' monks who were trying to modernize monastic practice in a non-contemplative direction. Merton wanted no part of that: his was a traditional monasticism centred on contemplation and he hoped to find connection with the Dalai Lama in a conversation on the mystical life.

When 4 November arrived, Merton's audience with the Dalai Lama both belied and exceeded his expectations. Afterwards, Merton recalled how impressive and charismatic the Dalai Lama was, and how the 'solidity' of the Tibetans 'counteract[ed] the bizarre reports about some of their practices'. The meeting went so well that two more appointments would follow on 6 and 8 November. After their final meeting, Merton virtually gushed with excitement: the Dalai Lama had praised him as a 'Catholic *geshe*' (the equivalent of a doctoral degree in Tibetan monastic education), and Merton called them 'very good friends'. For Merton, the meeting with the Dalai Lama turned out to be deeply significant, especially 'in the way we were able to communicate with one another and share an essentially spiritual experience of "Buddhism" which is also somehow in harmony with Christianity'. These were among the final words that Merton would write: only thirty-two days later, he died by accidental electrocution in Thailand, where he was attending an interfaith conference on monasticism.

The Dalai Lama would later recall his meeting with Thomas Merton in similar glowing terms. In calling him a 'Catholic *geshe*', the Dalai Lama recognized Merton's role as 'a strong bridge between our two very different religious traditions'. Merton had helped the Dalai Lama recognize the 'many similarities between Buddhism and Catholicism'. And yet, the Dalai Lama's recollection of their encounter also diverged in crucial respects. While Merton in his journal had emphasized their conversations about the inner mystical life, the Dalai Lama remembered their discussion of physical posture and breathing as 'vital components' to the practice of meditation. This stands in stark contrast to Merton, who had viewed bodily practices and 'traditional forms of cult and observance ... as relatively secondary'.

I recount this famous meeting between Merton and the Dalai Lama because it encapsulates important aspects of the role that monasticism has played in the modern religious landscape with respect to mobility, dialogue, and cultural exchange. In the late 20th and early 21st centuries, the relative ease of travel—both physical and virtual—has opened up new opportunities for interreligious encounters. And yet such moments of encounter are by no means simple: they involve rather subtle and complex negotiations of similarity and difference.

Thus, even as Merton and the Dalai Lama wrote about the 'harmony' and compatibility of Christian and Buddhist monasticism, they each took it on assumption as the basis for their conversations that these two 'religions' were separate, discrete, and bounded entities in the world. At the intersection of their contemplative concerns, it is notable that on occasion they playfully crisscrossed this boundary. Thus, in Dharamsala, the Dalai Lama honoured Merton by calling him a 'Catholic *geshe*'. Deeply influenced by D. T. Suzuki and the importation of Zen Buddhism to North America in the 1960s, Merton himself had already begun experimenting with Chinese and Japanese philosophies of silence, stillness, and emptiness before his visit with the Dalai Lama. Five years earlier, he had written in a letter to a friend, 'I think that I am as much a Chinese Buddhist in temperament and spirit as I am a Christian...I think one can certainly believe in the revealed truths of Christianity and follow Christ, while at the same time having a Buddhist outlook on life and nature.'

Such rhetorical border-crossings had the function of temporarily disrupting the seemingly discrete categories of Buddhism and Christianity, but in the end neither Merton nor the Dalai Lama was willing to abandon their reliance on an underlying world religions model with its associated global geographies of East and West. Both notably embraced a form of dialogue founded on allegiance to one's own religious and monastic tradition and rejected a 'loose and irresponsible syncretism' or a 'synthesis' that might obscure differences between religions.

In many ways, the meeting between these Christian and Buddhist monks, Thomas Merton and the 14th Dalai Lama, was an iconic moment in the making of modern religion. On the one hand, even as they endorsed the benefits of contemplative exchange and dialogue, Merton and the Dalai Lama were interested in vigorously reinforcing the integrity and boundedness of their own religious traditions. On the other hand, even as they resisted the dangers of so-called 'syncreticism' and 'synthesis', their meeting hints at the potential for other kinds of monastic border-crossings—and the production of other hybridized forms of monasticism—in the late 20th and early 21st centuries.

In what follows, I survey four case studies of such hybridity. The first involves the appeal to historical monastic practice as a means of validating Scientology as a new modern 'religion'. The second is the surprising emergence of various Protestant monastic communities, including Taizé and the so-called New Monasticism. The third concerns certain kinds of 'interspiritual' monastic practice, where the boundaries between 'world religions' are intentionally blurred and elided. The fourth, the Art Monastery Project, involves a blend of artistic and contemplative practice. In each context, monastic legacies have been appropriated in the creation of new, hybridized forms of religious community, and monasticism itself—in its disparate (post)modern forms—has been materially transformed through the 'cultural logic of globalization'.

The role that monasticism has played in the making of modern religion may be seen clearly in the case of Scientology, a movement founded by L. Ron Hubbard in the 1950s on the basis of his theory of Dianetics. From its inception, the Church of Scientology has been the subject of controversy, drawing bans and lawsuits in

Europe as an illegal sect, and public criticism in North America as a religious cult. Its Sea Organization—an inner circle of devoted disciples who sign contracts for a billion years of service and travel the globe as part of a private naval fleet—has drawn special attention for its secrecy and tight control over the flow of information. Indeed, the sequestering of its membership and its rigorous system of rules and requirements have been likened to forms of monastic community.

These comparisons are not incidental: rather, they have played a crucial role for the Scientologists themselves in their public self-representation and self-defence as a legitimized 'church' and 'world religion'. Thus, already in 1966, their founder, L. Ron Hubbard, wrote that 'in case of any challenge to the validity and religious nature of our Ethics system, Scientologists should refer to the example of early Buddhist monastic rules'. The official Scientology website underscores this connection, representing the Sea Organization as a 'religious order' comparable to Buddhist and Christian monastic communities in its system of vows and communal life:

> The billion-year vow of the Sea Organization member parallels almost exactly the Vow of Infinite Compassion of the one who undertakes to become a Bodhisattva in Mahayana Buddhism…This pattern in the history of the Church of Scientology parallels the formation of the first monastic sangha around Gautama Buddha, the first monks who followed St. Benedict, and the first Jesuit community that formed around St. Ignatius of Loyola…The Sea Organization is vital to the survival of Scientology as a world religion.

Here we see monastic rules and community organization appropriated as markers of legitimacy for a quintessentially modern religious movement—a movement that has experienced exponential growth but whose historical roots and ethical practices continue to be the subject of intense scrutiny.

Monastic models and practices have been appropriated in other rather unexpected contemporary religious contexts. I began this chapter by recalling the Protestant Reformation and its early modern cultural war against monasticism as a form of religious decadence and disunity. But the last seventy-five years or so have notably witnessed the emergence of vibrant, new forms of Protestant and Evangelical monasticism.

Perhaps the best-known example is Taizé, a Protestant monastic community established in eastern France during World War II. Its origins can be traced to the work of Roger Schutz—now remembered simply as Brother Roger—who grew up the son of a Swiss Reformed pastor and who studied theology in Strasbourg and Lausanne before he and some friends established an intentional community (La Grande Communauté) dedicated to prayer, silence, meditation, confession, discussion, and Bible study. In 1940, as the war raged on, the group purchased a house in the village of Taizé, just ten kilometres north of Cluny. There, they provided shelter to Jewish refugees from the occupied areas of France, and after the cessation of fighting they worked for reconciliation between the local French inhabitants and German prisoners of war.

The community at Taizé quickly embraced a distinctively monastic sense of identity. Brother Roger had written his master's thesis on the rule of St Benedict and expressed his vision for the monastic communal life in terms rather similar to the values embodied in the Cistercian reform movement, emphasizing work, rest, the Word of God, silence, joy, simplicity, and mercy as guiding values. The brothers living there adhere to their own rather simple set of vows, which emphasize renunciation of possessions, a commitment to celibacy, and obedience to the prior. Brother Roger filled this leadership role until his death in 2005 at the venerable age of ninety, when he was tragically assassinated by someone attending one of Taizé's worship gatherings.

For sixty-five years under Brother Roger's leadership, the Taizé community grew in both numbers and cultural influence. Despite its Protestant roots, it received endorsements from the archbishop of Lyons and Pope John XXIII, and Brother Roger was invited as an observer to the Second Vatican Council in 1962. Around the same time, Thomas Merton himself wrote a piece on 'Protestant Monasticism' in which he recognized and celebrated the irony 'that the Reformation which began by demolishing a whole segment of the tottering monastic fabric should now be seeking to help us rebuild it'. Meanwhile, the community at Taizé became a rapidly burgeoning pilgrimage centre for youth and young adults from all denominations and traditions. By the late 1980s, the annual number of visitors exceeded 100,000. Mother Teresa and Pope John Paul II paid visits, hundreds of lay volunteers stayed for designated periods to work and serve the needs of travellers, and groups of Catholic nuns took up residence nearby and partnered in the work of hospitality. Finally, the Taizé community's reach was extended through the exportation and popularization of the simple chanted songs and prayers they developed for their worship. Today, the repeated refrains of 'Cantate Domino' and 'Ubi Caritas' are heard in Protestant, Catholic, and Orthodox churches across the globe. In this way, through their liturgy and music, the French Protestant monks at Taizé have reintroduced a monastic ethos into modern Christian congregational life.

Taizé is by no means the only manifestation of Protestant monasticism in the modern world. Other intentional communities have sprung up in Taizé's wake. Some of them take less traditional forms, embodied for example in attempts to integrate both single and married persons, and even children, into their common life. One such group is the Anglican Order of Preachers, 'a religious community of men and women, lay and ordained, celibate and married, committed to the Dominican path of Christian Discipleship'.

A global phenomenon in the contemporary world

Two others are the Rutba House in Durham, North Carolina, and the Knights of Prayer™ Monastic Order in Portland, Oregon. Both represent countercultural Evangelical communities identified with an ecumenical movement known as 'New Monasticism'. In the case of the Rutba House, members dedicate themselves to twelve 'marks' that characterize their common life, akin to a set of rules or vows. These include certain recognizable monastic virtues such as the sharing of economic resources, hospitality, peacemaking, and contemplation. The Knights of Prayer™ identify themselves as part of 'a worldwide lay monastic community' consisting of 'only born-again Christians' and requiring 'no formal vows or lifetime commitment'. All that is required is agreement with a markedly evangelical statement of faith, a prescribed course of study, observance of daily hours of prayer, participation in prayer chain requests, and a monthly contribution: $30 per month or more will earn those who are 'already monks in their hearts' a Monastic Registration Wall Certificate and a wallet-sized Registration Card.

In Reading, England, another of these 'New Monastic' communities has purchased and occupied a previously abandoned medieval Benedictine abbey. Its founder Andy Freeman co-authored the book, *Punk Monk*. In it he narrates his life journey from a dissolute garage band member to his role in establishing a 'third millennium monastery' called the 'Boiler Room', which sponsors 24/7 prayer practices and strives to integrate contemporary art and music into worship gatherings. Freeman's book is full of references to the lives of early Christian monastic exemplars like Benedict, Pachomius, and the desert fathers, and he is keen to summon the pious presence of the Benedictine monks who inhabited the abbey centuries before. From Taizé to the New Monastics, we see how latter-day Protestants have sought in various ways to connect with a reclaimed Christian monastic past: through rituals of praying and chanting, through study of church fathers and mothers, and through the reinhabitation of sacred space.

In these examples, what we witness is a variegated landscape of 'new monasticisms' (plural), but this landscape is by no means populated only by Protestant or Evangelical Christian communities. Indeed, many such renewal movements embrace more diverse and hybrid religious identities, sometimes identifying themselves as 'interspiritual'. An early forerunner of such communities was established by a Benedictine monk named Bede Griffiths: from 1968 until his death in 1993 he oversaw a Christian-Hindu ashram in India, which he understood as 'the extension of the monastic ideal to lay groups'. In the 1980s, Betty Lanzetta founded a 'Community of the New Monastic Way', which participates in 'multi-faith and interspiritual conversations' and strives to operate 'outside of the monastic enclosure and even outside of a religious denomination'. Her 2005 book, *Radical Wisdom*, expands on her vision for a 'contemplative feminism' inspired by the female mystics of medieval Europe, especially Teresa of Avila.

Other forms of 'interspiritual' monasticism have proliferated as well. The Osage Forest of Peace in Sand Springs, Oklahoma—originally founded by a small group of nuns from the Benedictine Sisters of Perpetual Adoration—follows Bede Griffiths' model of a 'monastic ashram'. Their chapel in Sand Springs serves as an 'interspiritual, contemplative retreat center' for people from all traditions, including Buddhists, Hindus, and Muslims. The physical layout of the chapel reflects the community's interfaith practice. A sunken area in the middle evokes the Sundance Circle of the Osage Native American tribe. Above it, a cosmic wheel with eight spokes represents the eightfold Noble Path of Buddhism.

Such practices have been promoted through publications and the production of 'an interspiritual manifesto'. According to authors Rory McEntee and Adam Bucko, interspiritual New Monasticism is characterized by two shifts in focus that differentiate it from traditional practice: first, an eschewal of monastic withdrawal through a concerted commitment to engage with the world (in service to the poor and the environment); and second, the renunciation of renunciation through openness to a fuller spectrum of sexual and economic conditions beyond celibacy and poverty. One hallmark of this kind of 'interspiritual' monasticism is a recognition that holiness is to be found in the secular and that religiosity comes to expression in and through a range of vocations, whether contemplative, ecological, artistic, or administrative.

This leads me to my last case study of hybridity: the Art Monastery Project, which presents itself as a 'secular' blend of artistic and monastic practice. An international non-profit founded by artists Betsy McCall and Christopher Fülling, the Project sponsors retreats and laboratories modelled after 'the monastic principles of discipline, contemplation, and sustainable living'. From 2012 to 2015, it hosted a series of Art Monastic Laboratories at sites of former monasteries in Italy before shifting location to rural Vermont in 2016. These 'laboratories' have followed the temporal cycle of the Western monastic offices, or the 'liturgy of the hours', beginning with Vigils (night) in 2012, and proceeding through Sext (the sixth hour) in 2016. The sequence will continue with the prayer-hour themes of None (ninth hour), Vespers (sunset), and Compline (before sleep).

This ritualized pattern provides the context for an annual gathering ('Art Monastic Cycle') that allows participants (called Artmonks) to focus on 'research, dialogue, art making, and contemplation'. The Art Monastic Laboratories are also supplemented by week-long summer Artmonk Retreats and regular local meetings in northern California called the San Francisco Sangha, a name that draws directly on Buddhist notions of monastic community. Unlike many of the evangelical and interspiritual forms of New Monasticism, however, the Art Monastery Project conspicuously and persistently resists religious self-definition. Instead, it emphasizes the 'economic efficiencies' of intentional community and views monasticism 'less like something spiritual and more like a type of technology…for stable community and material support, as well as the sublime'. Still, in this seemingly post-religious, secular monasticism, we encounter a community markedly steeped in religious discourses and practices.

In these examples, we have encountered a diversified (post)modern landscape, where monasticism has sometimes come to be radically redefined. And yet, these new forms of monastic practice continue to engage in what should now be familiar as ritualized acts of social differentiation. In particular, we have seen how historical monastic models have been repurposed for new ends, transported across geographical and conceptual borders, and channelled through new media. In each case, communities seek to balance the value of historical monastic traditions with an impulse towards innovation and adaptation in responding to the particular challenges of an increasingly fast-paced, global world.

What difference then does monasticism make in modernity? In fact, it makes lots and lots of differences, resulting in many stripes and flavours of monastic practice. That's not to say that traditional forms of monasticism do not continue to flourish. They do. And in many countries, historical monasteries are booming, with burgeoning populations of monks and nuns seeking a life of renunciation and withdrawal—and with increasing numbers of devoted visitors and pious pilgrims insistently intruding upon their quietude. These communities are hemmed in by a world that leaves them less and less space to operate.

Thus, even the famously reclusive Carthusian monastic brothers at Grande Chartreuse high in the French Alps have seen fit to allow a filmmaker and his camera access to their cells and inner chambers. The result was the documentary *Into Great Silence* (2005) directed by Philip Gröning. It runs for over two and a half hours with hardly any dialogue or commentary: instead, it shows mute scenes of the monks walking, praying, and working, interspersed with close-ups of their serene eyes and faces. The only interview is a quiet conversation about time and God's providence with an elderly blind monk whose hoary eyebrows have grown long over his lids.

And yet, the lens of the camera is capable of penetrating otherwise inaccessible spaces, and its audio sensor pierces the silence by capturing the background noises of everyday monastic life—the tweeting of birds and the buzzing of flies heard through open windows, the clanking of wooden spoons on metal plates, the hum of electric razors shaving monks' scalps, the falling of rain or the dripping of water from a tap, the whisk of a broom or a mop, the opening and closing of doors, the shuffling of feet on wooden and stone floors, the tolling of the bell calling the monks to worship, the soft rustle of pages turned in a Bible, the sonorous Latin chanting of male voices echoing off the church walls and corridors, mellifluous liturgical words spoken in French, and the occasional free conversation on walks outside the monastery walls. The eye and ear of the camera bring the viewer into vicarious relationship with the members of the Grande Chartreuse community as they go about their daily business of being monks.

Halfway across the globe, a very different monastic community also became the subject of a documentary film when the 300 nuns living in the remote Kala Rongo Monastery (Nangchen, Tibet) welcomed filmmaker Bari Pearlman into their midst. Released in 2007 under the title *Daughters of Wisdom*, the film is narrated primarily in the voices of the Tibetan nuns themselves, who allow the camera to accompany them as they go about their chores—collecting and carrying buckets of water, tending to their gardens, harvesting plants, churning yak butter, making mud bricks, shopping for fruit and vegetables. They laugh and joke with one another, and reflect on their diverse and complicated relations with family. One cohabits with her father, mother, sister, and brother, who all followed her into the monastic life. A second zip lines across a wide river to receive lessons in the local village where she grew up and where her parents still live: now seventeen, she became a nun at age eleven. A third describes how her younger sister was prevented from becoming a nun due to the need to tend to her duties at her family's yak farm. A fourth shares the experience of undergoing a three-year retreat for new nuns, during which 'people from the outside weren't allowed to see us'. A fifth shares her thoughts on monasticism as a means of escaping women's suffering in childbirth. A sixth lives alone in a cave high on the steep cliffside overlooking the monastery: the photographer follows her into her hermitage and she shares her aversion to worldly life. In the film, the camera serves as a vestigial connection to that external world, but its gaze is also simply one more social obligation in a communal landscape already full of intricate familial and extra-familial ties.

The making of these documentaries brought two traditional monastic communities into contact with forms of global media that made them commodities for international viewing consumption. As viewers, we begin watching the films cognizant and self-conscious that we are strangers to their lives and intruders in their territories. But by the end, we realize how these monks and nuns, for years before our arrival, have already been living their lives at the intersection of silence and sound, of seclusion and society.

I began this book with a portrait of a Coptic monk, whose lament still echoes in my ears. 'The birds! Last night they were eating my brain!' With these words, he captured his own daily and nightly struggle with the push and pull of monastic solitude and communal engagement. Each day he works in the library and welcomes guests like me with a warm and genuine hospitality. Each night he returns alone to his cell where distracting thoughts afflict him. As such, he stands astride a perennial disjuncture—an internal division or split sense—in the monastic vocation. He has hit upon the place where monasticism in fact differs from itself. My monastic friend may be a solitary, but in these concerns and struggles he is certainly not alone. As we have seen in this *Very Short Introduction*, it is exactly where solitude and communal engagement come into collision that monasticism makes all the difference in the world.

References

Chapter 1: Definitions

Joseph Milner, *The History of the Church of Christ* (London: Merrill, 1794–1809).

Edwin A. Judge, 'The Earliest Use of *Monachos* for "Monk" and the Origins of Monasticism,' *Jahrbuch für Antike und Christentum* 20 (1977), 72–89, at 73.

Jerome, *Epistle 22, to Eustochium*: *NPNF*, ser. 2, vol. 6 (Peabody: Hendrickson, 1994), 37–8.

The Rule of the Master, trans. L. Eberle (Kalamazoo: Cistercian, 1977), 105–11.

The Rule of St. Benedict, trans. A. Meisel and M. del Mastro (Garden City: Image, 1975), 47.

Donald S. Lopez, Jr, *Buddhist Scriptures* (London: Penguin, 2004), 223–9, at 223 (adapted).

Vinaya Piṭaka: trans. I. Horner, *The Book of the Discipline*, 6 vols (London: Pali Text Society, 1949–66).

Eight Revered Precepts: I. Horner, *Women Under Primitive Buddhism* (London: Routledge, 1930), 118–61.

Jacques Derrida, 'Faith and Knowledge: The Two Sources of "Religion" at the Limits of Reason Alone,' in *Religion*, ed. J. Derrida and G. Vattimo (Stanford: Stanford University Press, 1998), 1–78.

Nirmala Salgado, *Buddhist Nuns and Gendered Practice* (Oxford: Oxford University Press, 2013), 3.

Philo of Alexandria: *Philo, Volume IX*, trans. F. Colson (Loeb Classical Library 363; Cambridge, MA: Harvard University Press, 1941), 54–5, 62–3, 112–15, 436–7, 442–3.

Genesis Rabbah XVII.2: trans. H. Freedman and M. Simon, *Midrash Rabbah*, 2 vols (London: Soncino, 1939), I.131.

Qur'ān, Surah 57:27 (my translation).

Malise Ruthven, *Islam in the World* (New York: Oxford University Press, 1984), 166.

Chapter 2: Differences

Catherine Bell, *Ritual Theory, Ritual Practice* (New York: Oxford University Press, 1992), 74, 100.

Patrick Olivelle, trans., *Upaniṣads* (New York: Oxford University Press, 1996), 68 and 270.

Patrick Olivelle, *Saṃnyāsa Upaniṣads* (New York: Oxford University Press, 1992), 43.

Raj Pruthi and Bela Rani Sharma, *Buddhism, Jainism and Women* (New Delhi: Anmol, 1995), 57.

Life of St. Anthony: trans. R. Gregg, in *Athanasius: The Life of Antony and the Letter to Marcellinus* (New York: Paulist, 1980), 29–99.

The Life of Simeon Stylites: trans. R. Doran (Kalamazoo: Cistercian, 1992).

Max Weber, *Economy and Society* (Berkeley: University of California Press, 1978).

The Rule of St. Benedict, trans. A. Meisel and M. del Mastro, 30, 45.

Philip Carr-Gomm, *A Brief History of Nakedness* (London: Reaktion, 2010), 56–62.

Jogye Order: <http://www.koreanbuddhism.net>.

John Holt, 'Sri Lanka: History', *EM* 2, 1198–1202, at 1198.

Chapter 3: Rules, social organization, and gender

Bentley Layton, 'Rules, Patterns, and the Exercise of Power in Shenoute's Monastery,' *Journal of Early Christian Studies* 15.1 (2007), 45–73, at 59.

Suzannah Hills, 'Hair Today, Gone Tomorrow: Young Monks Cry as Their Heads Are Shaved for Their Initiation into Buddhist Order,' *Daily Mail.com*, 13 May 2012, at <http://www.dailymail.co.uk/news/article-2144012/Young-monks-south-Korea-heads-shaved-initiation-Buddhist-order.html>.

Ludwig Wittgenstein, *Philosophical Investigations*, trans. G. Anscombe (Oxford: Wiley-Blackwell, 1991), par. 241.

Giorgio Agamben, *The Highest Poverty: Monastic Rules and Form-of-Life*, trans. A. Kotsko (Stanford: Stanford University Press, 2013), xi and 34 (quoting Mazon).

Donald S. Lopez, Jr, *Buddhist Scriptures* (London: Penguin, 2004), 230–51.

Pachomian *Precepts*: trans. A. Veilleux, *Pachomian Koinonia*, vol. 2 (Kalamazoo: Cistercian, 1981), 145–67.

Bentley Layton, *The Canons of Our Fathers: Monastic Rules of Shenoute* (Oxford: Oxford University Press, 2014), 78, 92–341.

Arnold van Gennep, *The Rites of Passage*, trans. M. Vizedom and G. Caffee (Chicago: University of Chicago Press, 1960).

Victor W. Turner, 'Betwixt and Between: The Liminal Period in *Rites de Passage*,' *The Proceedings of the American Ethnological Society* (1964), 4–20.

Gregory Schopen, *Buddhist Monks and Business Matters* (Honolulu: University of Hawai'i Press, 2004).

Bhikkhu Pātimokkha: ed. W. Pruitt, *The Pātimokkha*, trans. K. Norman (Oxford: Pali Text Society, 2001), 2–111.

Jean-Paul Sartre, *Being and Nothingness*, trans. H. Barnes (New York: Washington Square, 1943/56), 101–2.

Erving Goffman, *The Presentation of Self in Everyday Life* (New York: Doubleday, 1959), 75.

Bhikkhunī Pātimokkha, ed. W. Pruitt, 112–251.

Salgado, *Buddhist Nuns*, 2.

Greek *Life of Pachomius* 12: trans. A. Veilleux, *Pachomian Koinonia*, vol. 1 (Kalamazoo: Cistercian, 1980), 297–407, at 305.

Pachomian *Precepts*: trans. Veilleux, *Pachomian Koinonia*, vol. 2, 145–67.

Umberto Eco, *The Name of the Rose*, trans. W. Weaver (Boston: Mariner, 2014), 101.

Aline Rousselle, *Porneia: On Desire and the Body in Antiquity*, trans. F. Pheasant (Oxford: Blackwell, 1988), 155–6.

Tudor Sala, 'Dismantling Surveillance in Late Antique Corporate Monasticism,' PhD dissertation, Yale University, 2011.

Michel Foucault, *Discipline and Punish: The Birth of the Prison*, trans. A. Sheridan (New York: Vintage, 1977).

Chapter 4: Saints and spirituality

Life of Anthony, Introduction: trans. Gregg, 29.

Life of Saint Martin of Tours: NPNF, ser. 2, vol. 11, 3–17.

Robert L. Cohn, 'Sainthood,' in *Encyclopedia of Religion*, 2nd edition, vol. 12 (Detroit: Macmillan Reference USA, 2005), 8033–8, at 8033.

Kalpa Sutra 121: trans. H. Jacobi, *Gaina Sutras*, 2 vols (Oxford: Clarendon, 1884–95), I. 263–4.

Natubhai Shah, *Jainism*, vol. 1 (Brighton: Sussex Academic, 1998), 176.

Plato, *Republic* X.595–9: trans. A. Bloom, *The Republic of Plato* (New York: Basic, 1968), 277–82.

Aristotle, *Poetics* VI.2: trans. S. Butcher, *The Poetics of Aristotle*, 3rd edition (London: Macmillan, 1902), 23.

Edith Wyschogrod, *Saints and Postmodernism* (Chicago: University of Chicago Press, 1990), 13.

Ugolino Brunforte, *The Flowers of St. Francis* 1.1: trans. R. Brown (New York: Doubleday, 1958), 41.

Sayings of the Desert Fathers (Anonymous): ed. F. Nau, 'Histoire des solitaires égyptiens,' *Revue de l'orient chrétien* 13 (1908), 280 (= N 210).

Athanasius, *Life of Anthony* 47.1, trans. Gregg, 66.

Kalpa Sutra: trans. H. Jacobi, in *Gaina Sutras*, I. <I. 217–85.> 217–85.

Mahapadana Sutta: trans. T. and C. Rhys Davids, in *Dialogues of the Buddha*, part 2 (Oxford: Oxford University Press, 1910), 4–41.

Vividhatīrthakalpa 22 and 51: trans. P. Granoff, in *Speaking of Monks* (Oakville: Mosaic, 1992), 3, 12–13, 15–17.

John Kieschnick, *The Eminent Monk* (Honolulu: University of Hawai'i Press, 1997), 5, 39–40.

Peter Khoroche, trans., *Once the Buddha Was a Monkey: Ārya Śūra's Jātakamālā* (Chicago: University of Chicago Press, 1989).

Elizabeth Castelli, *Imitating Paul* (Louisville: Westminster/John Knox, 1991), 22.

Sayings of the Desert Fathers (Systematic): trans. J. Wortley, *The Book of the Elders* (Collegeville, MN: Liturgical, 2012), 233–45, at 235 (14.9) and 244 (14.31).

'The Monk Sukośala': trans. P. Granoff, in *The Forest of Thieves and the Magic Garden* (London: Penguin, 1998/2006), 49–56.

René Girard, 'Mimesis and Violence,' in *The Girard Reader*, ed. J. Williams (New York: Crossroad, 1996), 9–19, at 12.

Brian D. Robinette, 'Deceit, Desire, and the Desert: René Girard's Mimetic Theory in Conversation with Early Christian Monastic

Practice', in *Violence, Transformation, and the Sacred*, ed. M. Pfeil and T. Winright (Maryknoll: Orbis, 2012), 130–43, at 132.

Peter Brown, 'The Rise and Function of the Holy Man in Late Antiquity', in *Society and the Holy in Late Antiquity* (Berkeley: University of California Press, 1982), 103–52, at 131.

Peter Brown, *Authority and the Sacred* (Cambridge: Cambridge University Press, 1995), 75.

Life of Anthony: trans. Gregg, *passim*.

Gregory Nazianzen, *Oration* 21.5: *NPNF*, vol. 7, 270.

Johannes Quasten, *Patrology*, vol. 3 (Westminster: Christian Classics, 1992), 40.

Augustine, *Confessions*, Book 8: trans. R. Pine-Coffin (New York: Penguin, 1961), 157–79, esp. 166–8 (= 8.6) and 177–9 (= 8.12).

Mahinda Deegalle, 'Monasticism, Definitions of: Buddhist Perspectives', *EM* 2, 868–71, at 870.

Andrew Quintman, *The Yogin and the Madman: Reading the Biographical Corpus of Tibet's Great Saint Milarepa* (New York: Columbia University Press, 2014), 28, 44, 49, 168, 169, and 247, note 13.

Tsangnyön Heruka, *Life of Milarepa*: trans. A. Quintman (New York: Penguin, 2010), *passim*.

Life of Orgyan Chokyi: trans. K. Schaeffer, *Himalayan Hermitess* (Oxford: Oxford University Press, 2004).

Chapter 5: Spaces real and imagined

Sister Ann Marie Wainright, 'Home is Where the Heart Is': <http://www.duluthbenedictines.org/home-is-where-the-heart-is>.

Sayings of the Desert Fathers (Alphabetic): trans. B. Ward (Kalamazoo: Cistercian, 1975), 139.

Lopez, *Buddhist Scriptures*, 287.

Life of St. Benedict 1.3–8 and 2.1–5: trans. T. Kardong (Collegeville: Liturgical, 2009), 7–9, 13–14.

Life of Anthony 12: trans. Gregg, 40–42.

Bohairic *Life of Pachomius* 17: trans. Veilleux, *Pachomian Koinonia*, vol. 1, 39–40.

Bhikkhu Pātimokkha: ed. Pruitt, 51.

John Huntington and Chaya Chandrasekhar, 'Architecture: Buddhist Monasteries in Southern Asia', *EM* 1, 55–66, at 56.

Wlodzimierz Godlewski, 'Excavating the Ancient Monastery at
    Naqlun,' in *Christianity and Monasticism in the Fayoum Oasis*, ed.
    G. Gabra (Cairo: AUC Press, 2005), 155–71, esp. 157–8.

Alessandro Scafi, 'Pilgrimage to the Latin West: Subiaco,' in *Christian
    Pilgrimage, Landscape, and Heritage*, ed. A. Maddrell et al.
    (New York: Routledge, 2015), 91–128.

Huntington and Chandrasekhar, 'Architecture,' *EM* 1, 62.

James Caswell, 'Architecture: Structural Monasteries in East Asia,'
    EM 1, 72–7, at 76.

Senake Bandaranayake, *Sinhalese Monastic Architecture* (Leiden:
    Brill, 1974), 34.

Antoine Guillaumont et al., 'Kellia,' in *The Coptic Encyclopedia*, vol. 5
    (New York: Macmillan, 1991), 1396b–1410a.

Philip McWilliams, 'Architecture: Western Christian Monasteries,'
    EM 1, 77–82, at 77.

Christopher Brooke, *The Age of the Cloister* (New York: Paulist Press,
    2001), 173.

Sayings of the Desert Fathers (Alphabetic), trans. Ward, 3.

Brown, *Authority and the Sacred*, 76.

Richard Krautheimer, *Early Christian and Byzantine Architecture*,
    4th edition (New Haven: Yale University Press, 1986), 143–51.

McWilliams, 'Architecture: Western Christian Monasteries,' *EM* 1, 82.

John Jorgensen, 'Hagiography: Buddhist Perspectives,' in *EM* 1, 563–4,
    at 563.

Sculpture from Bodhgaya: New York, Rubin Museum of Art, C2005.4.2,
    HAR65388; <http://rubinmuseum.org/collection/artwork/
    major-events-of-the-buddhas-life>.

Huntington and Chandrasekhar, 'Architecture,' *EM* 1, 59.

John Huntington, 'Maṇḍala,' *EM* 2, 800–15, at 812.

Lindsay Jones, 'Architectural Catalysts to Contemplation,' in
    Transcending Architecture, ed. J. Bermudez (Washington, DC:
    Catholic University of America Press, 2015), 170–207, at 194.

Shitao, *Light of Dawn on the Monastery* (1669 CE), ink and wash
    painting. Public domain: <https://www.wikiart.org/en/shitao/
    light-of-dawn-on-the-monastery-1669>.

James Robson, 'Monastic Spaces and Sacred Traces,' in *Buddhist
    Monasticism in East Asia*, ed. J. A. Benn et al. (New York:
    Routledge, 2010), 43–64, esp. 48 and 52–3.

Mamoru Tonami, *The Shaolin Monastery Stele*, trans. P. Herbert
    (Kyoto: Italian School of East Asian Studies, 1990), 32.

Life of Onnophrius: trans. T. Vivian, in *Journeying into God* (Minneapolis: Fortress, 1996), 166–87.

Paul Meyvaert, 'The Medieval Monastic Garden,' in *Medieval Gardens*, ed. E. MacDougall (Washington, DC: Dumbarton Oaks, 1986), 23–53, esp. 50–3.

The Letters of Hildegard of Bingen, trans. J. Baird and R. Ehrman, vol. 1 (New York: Oxford University Press, 1994), 3–4.

E. A. W. Budge, *The Paradise of the Holy Fathers*, 2 vols (London: Oxford University Press, 1907; 2nd edition 1934).

David R. Keller, *Oasis of Wisdom: The Worlds of the Desert Fathers and Mothers* (Collegeville: Liturgical, 2005).

Chapter 6: A global phenomenon in the contemporary world

Martin Luther, 'On the Monastic Vows': trans. J. Atkinson, in *Luther's Worlds*, vol. 1 (Philadelphia: Fortress, 1966).

John Calvin, *Institutes of the Christian Religion*, 2 vols, ed. J. McNeill, trans. F. Battles (Philadelphia: Westminster, 1960).

Jack Tannous, 'Qenneshre, Monastery of,' in *Gorgias Encyclopedic Dictionary of the Syriac Heritage*, ed. S. Brock et al. (Piscataway: Gorgias, 2011), 345–6.

Benedict Anderson, *Imagined Communities*, rev. ed. (London: Verso, 1991), esp. 9–10.

Ronald D. Schwartz, *Circle of Protest: Political Ritual in the Tibetan Uprising* (New Delhi: Moltilal Banarsidass, 1996), esp. 74–108, at 89.

Jason Szep, 'SPECIAL REPORT: Buddhist Monks Incite Muslim Killings in Myanmar,' *Reuters*, 8 April 2013; *al-Jazeera* documentary, 'Monks of War,' at <https://www.youtube.com/watch?v=a5IhiF6KFyQ&spfreload=10>.

Rohini Mohan, 'Sri Lanka's Violent Buddhists,' *New York Times*, 2 January 2015.

Michelle Boorstein, 'The Nuns on the Bus Tour Promotes Social Justice—and Turns a Deaf Ear to the Vatican,' *Washington Post*, 27 June 2012.

Meghan Trainor, 'All About That Bass': music video at <http://www.youtube.com/watch?v=7PCkvCPvDXk>.

'#NunTrouble: It's All About That Bus': music video at <http://www.youtube.com/watch?v=In-glzIs5jI>.

Talal Asad, *Genealogies of Religion* (Baltimore: Johns Hopkins University Press, 1993), chapters 1 and 5.

Thomas Merton, *The Seven Storey Mountain* (Fiftieth Anniversary Edition; New York: Harvest, 1998).

Thomas Merton, *The Asian Journal of Thomas Merton*, ed. N. Burton et al. (New York: New Directions, 1968/75), 29–31, 92–3, 100–3, 112–13, 124–5, 148.

The Fourteenth Dalai Lama, *Freedom in Exile* (San Francisco: HarperSanFrancisco, 1990), 189–90.

Bonnie Thurston, ed., *On Eastern Meditation* (New York: New Directions, 2012), xiv.

Thomas Merton, *Mystics and Zen Masters* (New York: Farrar, Straus, and Giroux, 1961/7), 207.

The Fourteenth Dalai Lama, *A Policy of Kindness* (Ithaca: Snow Lion, 1990), 63–4.

Marwan Kraidy, *Hybridity, or the Cultural Logic of Globalization* (Philadelphia: Temple University Press, 2005).

Hugh Urban, *The Church of Scientology* (Princeton: Princeton University Press, 2011), 107, 125–6.

Frank K. Flinn, 'The Sea Organization and Its Role with the Church of Scientology,' White Paper (January 2010), section II, at <http://www.scientologyreligion.org/religious-expertises/the-SO-and-its-role>.

Jason Brian Santos, *A Community Called Taizé* (Downers Grove: IVP, 2008).

Merton, *Mystics and Zen Masters*, 188–92, at 192.

Anglican Order of Preachers: 'NAECC: The National Association of Episcopal Christian Communities,' <http://www.anglicandominicans.com>.

Rutba House: Jonathan Wilson Hartgrove, *New Monasticism: What It Has to Say to Today's Church* (Grand Rapids: Brazos, 2008).

Knights of Prayer™ Monastic Order: 'Worldwide Lay Monastic Community,' at <http://www.prayerfoundation.org/lay_monastic_community_portland.htm>.

Andy Freeman and Pete Greig, *Punk Monk: New Monasticism and the Ancient Art of Breathing* (Ventura: Regal, 2007), 53.

Bede Griffiths, 'The Extension of the Monastic Ideal to Lay Groups,' recorded lecture in *Christian Meditation: The Evolving Tradition*, volume 2 (The John Main Seminar, New Harmony, IN, 1991; Chevy Chase: The John Main Institute, 1991; reissued by Medio Media under the title, *The New Creation in Christ. Volume 2: The Extension of the Monastic Ideal to the Laity*).

Betty Lanzetta, *Radical Wisdom: A Feminist Mystical Theology* (Minneapolis: Fortress, 2005).

Osage Forest of Peace: <http://www.forestofpeace.org>.

Rory McEntee and Adam Bucko, *New Monasticism: An Interspiritual Manifesto for Contemplative Living* (Maryknoll: Orbis, 2015).

Art Monastery Project: <http://artmonastery.org>.

Film, *Into Great Silence* (dir. Philip Gröning, 2005; Zeitgeist Films, 2007).

Film, *Daughters of Wisdom* (dir. Bari Pearlman, 2007; BTG Productions, 2007).

Further reading

Chapter 1: Definitions

On varieties of ancient Christian monasticism: James Goehring, *Ascetics, Society, and the Desert* (Harrisburg: TPI, 1999); Susanna Elm, *Virgins of God* (Oxford: Clarendon, 1994).

On the life of the Buddha and early Buddhist monasticism: Aśvaghoṣa, *Life of the Buddha*, trans. P. Olivelle (New York: New York University Press, 2008); John Strong, *Buddhisms* (London: Oneworld, 2015); and Alice Collett, *Lives of Early Buddhist Nuns* (New Delhi: Oxford University Press, 2016).

On the Essenes and Therapeutae: John Collins, *Beyond the Qumran Community* (Grand Rapids: Eerdmans, 2010; Joan Taylor, *Jewish Women Philosophers of First-Century Alexandria* (Oxford: Oxford University Press, 2003), chs 1–7.

On Sufism: Julian Baldick, *Mystical Islam* (New York: New York University Press, 1989).

Chapter 2: Differences

On the *Upaniṣads*: Patrick Olivelle, *Early Upanisads* (New York: Oxford University Press, 1998).

On Mahāvīra: Paul Dundas, *The Jains*, 2nd edition (London: Routledge, 1992), 12–44.

On demons, illness, and health care in early Christian monasticism: David Brakke, *Demons and the Making of the Monk* (Cambridge, MA: Harvard University Press, 2006); Andrew Crislip, *From Monastery to Hospital* (Ann Arbor: University of Michigan Press, 2005).

On Western medieval orders and female communities: Brooke, *Age of the Cloister*; Jeffrey Hamburger and Susan Marti, eds., *Crown and Veil* (New York: Columbia University Press, 2008).

On Jain sects and Buddhist schools: Paul Dundas, *Jains*; Rupert Gethin, *The Foundations of Buddhism* (Oxford: Oxford University Press, 1998).

On Daoist monasticism: Livia Kohn, *Monastic Life in Medieval Daoism* (Honolulu: University of Hawai'i Press, 2003); Adeline Herrou, *A World of Their Own: Daoist Monks and Their Community in Contemporary China* (St Petersburg: Three Pines Press, 2013).

On Buddhist monasticism in China, Japan, Korea, and Tibet: relevant articles in *EM*.

Chapter 3: Rules, social organization, and gender

On resocialization and rites of passage: Peter Berger and Thomas Luckmann, *The Social Construction of Reality* (Garden City: Doubleday, 1967); Victor Turner, *The Ritual Process* (London: Penguin, 1969).

On the Sanskrit and Tibetan versions of the *Vinaya*: Charles Prebish, *Buddhist Monastic Discipline* (Delhi: Motilal Banarsidass, 1996/2002); Lopez, *Buddhist Scriptures*, 230–51.

On monastic rules about food: Bentley Layton, 'Social Structure and Food Consumption in an Early Christian Monastery,' *Le Muséon* 115.1–2 (2002), 25–55.

On the ban against women on Mount Athos: Alice-Mary Talbot, 'Women and Mt Athos,' in *Mount Athos and Byzantine Monasticism*, ed. A. Bryer and M. Cunningham (Brookfield: Variorum, 1996), 67–79.

Chapter 4: Saints and spirituality

On *jina*s, *arhat*s, and *bodhisattva*s: Shah, *Jainism*, vol. 1; George Bond, 'The Arahant: Sainthood in Theravāda Buddhism,' in *Sainthood*, ed. R. Kieckhefer and G. D. Bond (Berkeley: University of California Press, 1988), 140–71; Strong, *Buddhisms*.

On *mimēsis*: Stephen Halliwell, *The Aesthetics of Mimesis* (Princeton: Princeton University Press, 2002); Peter Brown, 'The Saint as Exemplar in Late Antiquity,' *Representations* 2 (1983), 1–25.

On karmic stories and exemplary biographies: Naomi Appleton, *Narrating Karma and Rebirth* (Cambridge: Cambridge University Press, 2014); Julie Schober, 'Trajectories in Buddhist Sacred Biography,' in *Sacred Biography in the Buddhist Traditions of South and Southeast Asia* (Honolulu: University of Hawai'i Press, 1997), 2–18.

Chapter 5: Spaces real and imagined

On 'adaptive reuse' and 'purpose-built' architecture: Darlene Brooks Hedstrom, 'Divine Architects: Designing the Monastic Dwelling Place,' in *Egypt in the Byzantine World 300–700*, ed. R. Bagnall (Cambridge: Cambridge University Press, 2007), 368–89.

On Buddhist rock-cut cave monasteries: James Caswell, 'Cave Temples and Monasteries in India and China,' in *EM* 1, 255–63; Benoy Behl, *The Ajanta Caves* (London: Thames and Hudson, 1998); Neville Agnew et al., eds, *Cave Temples of Dunhuang* (Los Angeles: Getty Conservation Institute, 2016).

On purpose-built Buddhist monasteries: Robin Coningham, 'The Archaeology of Buddhism,' in *Archaeology and World Religion*, ed. T. Insoll (London: Routledge, 2001), 61–95; Lars Fogelin, *Archaeology of Early Buddhism* (Lanham: Altamira, 2006).

On the Yale Monastic Archaeology Project: <http://egyptology.yale.edu/expeditions/current-expeditions>.

On the monastic cloister: Brooke, *Age of the Cloister*, esp. 70–85, 166–94.

On cosmic symbolism in Buddhist monastic architecture: Susan Huntington, with John Huntington, *Art of Ancient India* (New York: Weatherhill, 1985).

On maṇḍalas: Romi Khosla, 'Architecture and Symbolism in Tibetan Monasteries,' in *Shelter, Sign, and Symbol*, ed. P. Oliver (Woodstock: Overlook, 1975), 71–83; Martin Brauen et al., *Mandala* (New York: Rubin Museum of Art, 1997).

Chapter 6: A global phenomenon in the contemporary world

On King Henry VIII's dissolution of monastic properties: Peter Clery, *The Monastic Estate* (Felpham: Phillimore, 2015).

On the modern concept of 'religion': Brent Nongbri, *Before Religion* (New Haven: Yale University Press, 2013); Peter Beyer, 'Religion and Globalization,' in *The Blackwell Companion to Globalization*, ed. G. Ritzer (Oxford: Blackwell, 2007), 444–60.

On ancient Christian and modern Buddhist monastic acts of violence: Michael Gaddis, *There is No Crime for Those Who Have Christ: Religious Violence in the Christian Roman Empire* (Berkeley: University of California Press, 2005), 151–250; Michael Jerryson, *Buddhist Fury* (Oxford: Oxford University Press, 2011).

On Thomas Merton and Zen Buddhism: Robert Daggy, ed., *Encounter: Thomas Merton and D. T. Suzuki* (Monterey: Larkspur, 1988); 'A Hidden Wholeness: The Zen Photography of Thomas Merton', <http://www.merton.org/hiddenwholeness/>.

On 'Interspiritual' monasticism: Wayne Teasdale, *The Mystic Heart* (Novato: New World, 1999).

Index

Index

Monasticism

SOCIAL MEDIA
Very Short Introduction

Join our community

www.oup.com/vsi

- Join us online at the official Very Short Introductions **Facebook** page.
- Access the thoughts and musings of our authors with our online **blog**.
- Sign up for our monthly **e-newsletter** to receive information on all new titles publishing that month.
- Browse the full range of Very Short Introductions online.
- Read **extracts** from the Introductions for free.
- If you are a teacher or lecturer you can order inspection copies quickly and simply via our website.

KABBALAH
A Very Short Introduction
Joseph Dan

In *Kabbalah*, Joseph Dan debunks the myths surrounding modern Kabbalistic practice, offering an engaging and dependable account of this traditional Jewish religious phenomenon and its impact outside of Judaism. Dan sheds light on the many misconceptions about what Kabbalah is and isn't—including its connections to magic, astronomy, alchemy, and numerology—and he illuminates the relationship between Kabbalah and Christianity on the one hand and New Age religion on the other. Dan examines its fascinating historical background, including key ancient texts of this tradition. He concludes with a brief survey of scholarship in the field and a list of books for further reading.

> "Dan has given us the best concise history of Jewish mysticism. . . . As a 'very short introduction' to this sublime treasure house, Joseph Dan's book is warmly recommended."
>
> Benjamin Balint, Commentary

www.oup.com/vsi

CHRISTIAN ETHICS
A Very Short Introduction
D. Stephen Long

This *Very Short Introduction* to Christian ethics introduces the topic by examining its sources and historical basis. D. Stephen Long presents a discussion of the relationship between Christian ethics, modern, and postmodern ethics, and explores practical issues including sex, money, and power. Long recognises the inherent difficulties in bringing together 'Christian' and 'ethics' but argues that this is an important task for both the Christian faith and for ethics. Arguing that Christian ethics are not a precise science, but the cultivation of practical wisdom from a range of sources, Long also discusses some of the failures of the Christian tradition, including the crusades, the conquest, slavery, inquisitions, and the Galileo affair.

www.oup.com/vsi

CATHOLICISM
A Very Short Introduction
Gerald O'Collins

Despite a long history of external threats and internal strife, the
Roman Catholic Church and the broader reality of Catholicism
remain a vast and valuable presence into the third millennium of
world history. What are the origins of the Catholic Church? How
has Catholicism changed and adapted to such vast and diverse
cultural influences over the centuries? What great challenges
does the Catholic Church now face in the twenty-first century,
both within its own life and in its relation to others around the
world? In this Very Short Introduction, Gerald O'Collins draws on
the best current scholarship available to answer these questions
and to present, in clear and accessible language, a fresh
introduction to the largest and oldest institution in the world.

PAGANISM
A Very Short Introduction
Owen Davies

This *Very Short Introduction* explores the meaning of paganism - through a chronological overview of the attitudes towards its practices and beliefs - from the ancient world through to the present day. Owen Davies largely looks at paganism through the eyes of the Christian world, and how, over the centuries, notions and representations of its nature were shaped by religious conflict, power struggles, colonialism, and scholarship. Despite the expansion of Christianity and Islam, Pagan cultures continue to exist around the world, whilst in the West new formations of paganism constitute one of the fastest-growing religions.

www.oup.com/vsi

RELIGION IN AMERICA

A Very Short Introduction

Timothy Beal

Timothy Beal describes many aspects of religion in contemporary America that are typically ignored in other books on the subject, including religion in popular culture and counter-cultural groups; the growing phenomenon of "hybrid" religious identities, both individual and collective; the expanding numbers of new religious movements, or NRMs, in America; and interesting examples of "outsider religion." He also offers an engaging overview of the history of religion in America, from Native American traditions to the present day. Finally, Beal highlights the three major forces shaping the present and future of religion in America.